THE WEEK

T0382180

THE WEEK

AN ESSAY ON
THE ORIGIN & DEVELOPMENT OF
THE SEVEN-DAY CYCLE

By

F. H. COLSON, M.A.

Formerly Fellow of St John's College
Cambridge

CAMBRIDGE
AT THE UNIVERSITY PRESS
MCMXXVI

CAMBRIDGE
UNIVERSITY PRESS

University Printing House, Cambridge CB2 8BS, United Kingdom

Cambridge University Press is part of the University of Cambridge.

It furthers the University's mission by disseminating knowledge in the pursuit of education, learning and research at the highest international levels of excellence.

www.cambridge.org
Information on this title: www.cambridge.org/9781107486690

First published 1926
First paperback edition 2015

A catalogue record for this publication is available from the British Library

ISBN 978-1-107-48669-0 Paperback

PREFACE

THIS little book has at any rate the justification that it is the first or almost the first attempt to present the subject with any fullness to English readers. The only exception known to me is an article by Julius Hare on 'The Names of the Days of the Week,' in the *Philological Museum* of 1830. That article is longer than my own treatise and is distinguished throughout by great learning, but it covers very different ground, to say nothing of the fact that additional sources of knowledge have naturally become available in the course of almost a century. I myself wrote a few pages on the subject in the course of some notes on Justin Martyr in the *Journal of Theological Studies* of January, 1922, and at the end of these I remarked that I had met with no good monograph on the Week, and that what I had written was put forward as much in the hope of eliciting as of giving information. That hope has been disappointed, but since then I have come across a great deal of German work which has added much to my knowledge. Of this the most noteworthy items are substantial articles by Schürer, by Jensen and others and by Boll, to which references are given on pp. 20, 45 and 58. To these I might add Maass' *Tagesgötter*, though I have not had occasion to quote it.

The principal difference between my treatment and theirs lies in this—that I am more impressed, than they seem to be, with the feeling that the silent and unofficial diffusion of a new time-cycle through a vast empire is a very remarkable fact and that it argues some powerful motive behind it, and I have spent some effort in trying to arrive at some conception of what this motive was. Further this same feeling has led me to the belief that the Planetary Week, like Mithraism and the other mystery-religions, is an important factor in the background of primitive Christianity, and that its existence must not be ignored, especially when we consider the origin of the Christian Sunday. This aspect of the question is almost totally ignored by the scholars I have mentioned and indeed, I think, by nearly all the theologians who have examined with laborious and sometimes fanciful ingenuity the possible traces of the mystical beliefs of paganism in Christian theology and institutions. Some years ago I listened to a paper on this subject by an eminent divine now dead. I said to him afterwards, 'There is one thing you have not mentioned—the week.' He looked at me with surprise and said, 'Who do you mean by the weak?' When I explained that my word was spelt with an *e* he remained equally mystified.

While I have no illusions which would lead me to expect a wide circulation for the book, I do hope that outside the narrow circle of professional scholars, it may interest others here and there, who have the curiosity to know something about the history of an institution which governs their lives and the lives of most of the civilized nations. To such I have tried to make myself intelligible. All Greek and nearly all Latin have been banished from the body of the text and I have explained many points which to a good Classical scholar need no explanation. At the same time I hope that the latter will find that he is furnished with the references which will enable him to test the accuracy of what is stated as fact and the validity of the inferences drawn from the facts. That these inferences should meet with general agreement is more than I expect, indeed more than I wish. I would rather repeat in another form what I said in my earlier note mentioned above that I hope the book may stimulate a further enquiry into a subject which has to my mind been somewhat strangely neglected in this country.

F. H. C.

Cambridge
June 1926

CONTENTS

THE WEEK IN GENERAL

The standards of time-measurement which nature has given us are the year, the month and the day. Primitive observation discovered at an early date that a year was something between 365 and 366 days, and a month something between 29 and 30 days. The relation of year to day did not present much difficulty. Even the pre-Julian year of 365 days without leap-years would not produce much confusion in a single life-time. The introduction of an extra day once in four years set matters right for some centuries and the Gregorian reform by which three leap-years are omitted in four centuries will with very slight adaptation carry us on as long as the world is inhabited. So too by a system of alternations between 29 and 30 days, the month may be made to consist of a complete number of days and yet keep pace with the moon. But the relation of month to year was a more difficult proposition. Since 12 true months have approximately 354 days and 13 have 383, we have had to choose between reckoning by lunar months which run on independently of the year, and artificial months, a fixed number of which will complete the year.

c

In Europe we have chosen the second course, but at the price of parting with the moon, so that our 12 months, while forming a convenient subdivision of the year and an adequate guide to the seasons, have no relation to the planet from which they receive their name. We have also subdivided our day into hours and, at a later time, into minutes and seconds, arbitrary subdivisions indeed, but still forming a system, so that a year consists of a fixed number of complete months, a month of complete days, though in varying numbers, and days of a fixed number of complete hours.

Across this ordered system runs that intruder the week, consisting indeed of a fixed number of complete days, but paying no regard to months or years. The moment that begins a new year, begins also a new month, a new day, and a new hour, but only once in five years, at the least, a new week. It is very frequently and indeed, I think, generally assumed that this continuous week somehow represents the four phases of the moon. It is true that the course of the moon naturally to the eye of the observer groups itself into quarters and that if 29½ be divided by 4 the nearest integral number is 7 and the next nearest 8. It is also true that the three early varieties of the week, of which we have any knowledge, the Jewish, the Planetary, and the old Roman, consist of either seven or eight days. But at the same time it is obvious that continuous

weeks of either of these lengths would be of
no use to the moon observer. They would lead
him wrong at the very outset. The only way of
fitting a seven-day week into the lunar month
of 29 to 30 days, or for the matter of that into
the artificial month of 30 to 31 days, is to have
one week at least of the four longer than seven
days, or what is the same thing to intercalate
one or more days at the end of the four weeks.
Similarly an eight-day week can only be fitted
into the month by shortening one at least of the
four weeks. Of such a subdivisional or, as I will
for convenience call it, a 'lunar' week, there are
apparently traces in the primitive records of
Babylonia and of ancient Persia[1]. But the 'lunar'
week differs vitally from the continuous, and,
while it is possible that the latter may have been
developed from the former, I do not think the
possibility rises above the region of speculation.
The earliest forms of the continuous week of
which we have any knowledge were justified by
the nations which used them on grounds which
have nothing to do with the moon or the month.
There are, as I have said, three such forms, the
Roman, the Jewish and the Planetary.

The Roman usage, by which the nundinae[2],

---

[1] For Persia *v.* Ginzel, *Handbuch der mathematischen und
technischen Chronologie,* I, p. 281; also Hastings, *Encycl.
Religion and Ethics,* art. 'Calendar (Persian).'

[2] For information on the 'nundinae' *v. Dict. of Antiquities*
or, better, Marquardt, *Römische Staatsverwaltung,* III, p. 289.

or market-day, recurred every eighth day and thus produced a week which was marked on their calendars by the letters *a* to *h*, as our week is marked in the prayer-book calendar by the letters *a* to *g*, was always explained by them in the same way. The agriculturists worked in the fields for seven days and came into the city on the eighth to sell their produce. This explanation seems reasonable enough. The Jewish week, as we all know, was produced by the recurrence every seventh day of a 'sabbath,' that is a periodical abstention from work, believed to be enjoined by the Deity and observed in honour of him. Here the connexion of the Jews with Babylon and perhaps the fact that the earlier mentions of the Sabbath couple it with the New Moon give some plausibility to the view that it was developed out of the 'lunar' week. But this plausibility falls far short of certainty. If the belief that the Deity demands a 'sabbath' is once established, the needs of human life ensure that it should not recur at too frequent intervals. The Jews themselves had, of course, an explanation of the seven-day interval, which has no connexion with the 'lunar.' The antiquity of this explanation may be doubted, but apart from this the number seven is as likely as any other, and may have been determined by the sanctity which, whatever the cause, from early times adhered to this particular number[1].

[1] *V*. p. 56.

The planetary week rests on a different principle, namely, the idea that the whole of time is under the control of divine beings, each of whom rules in turn. In this case the length of the week is clearly determined by the number of the divine beings concerned. In the case of the planetary week, these divine beings are the planets[1], and therefore the number was fixed by nature. It is a fact of nature that the number of the planets visible to the ancients was seven, and this fact has no connexion with the phases of the moon or with the lunar week. While it is possible that there may be some prehistoric link between them, such a supposition is obviously quite unnecessary.

Closely connected with the question we have been discussing is the idea that the week is an institution of immemorial antiquity and general diffusion. If we identified the continuous week with the lunar, we might perhaps, in view of the somewhat meagre evidence from Babylonia, admit its great antiquity, though this would not prove its general diffusion. If we consider the connexion between the two forms of week to be problematical, we can only ascribe to the continuous week with any certainty such antiquity as we find in the Roman and Jewish institutions.

---

[1] To avoid any misconception, I may say once for all that throughout this treatise the word 'planet' is used in the ancient sense, to include sun and moon as well as what we now call the planets.

The planetary week, we shall find, cannot be traced to a date much prior to our era[1]. As for the diffusion, I have been able to find nothing outside these three, or what is derived from them. The Greeks of the Classical period certainly had no week of any kind. No trace of it seems to be found in ancient Egypt. The Persian week, as I have already noted, is of the 'lunar' type, consisting of two weeks of seven and two of eight days. The Indian planetary week, which seems in earlier times to have belonged to esoteric astrology rather than to popular usage, shews signs of being an offshoot of the later Greek, borrowed at a date subsequent to our era. Similarly the Teutonic week is borrowed from the later Roman. It is a matter of common knowledge that the Arabs under Mohammed learnt to observe one day in seven, namely, our Friday, as sacred, but whether anything of the sort existed in pre-Islamic Arabia is a point on which authorities appear to be divided[2]. But at any rate it does not appear that it can be traced back to a time earlier than that at which the Judaeo-Christian week was firmly established in the neighbouring countries.

I imagine indeed that the common belief in

[1] The probability or improbability of a remote origin for this type of week is discussed later, on pp. 55 ff.

[2] Ginzel (*Handbuch*, I, p. 242) says that it is pre-Islamic, but does not give any evidence as to the time to which it can be traced.

the primitiveness and universality of the week is
largely a survival from the idea, under which I
was myself brought up, that paganism was a corruption of revealed truth. Just as the various
legends of the Deluge were distortions of the
authentic story of Noah, so it was with the week.
God had created the world in six days and rested
on the seventh; and the descendants of Adam
had dimly remembered this, though they cor-
rupted it to idolatrous uses. Thus we used to be
told that the Anglo-Saxons gave the names of
their own deities to the days of the week. No
one asked how they came to have week-days to
name, for the week had been from the beginning.
Conversely the supposed antiquity and universality of the week was used to confirm the
Mosaic record[1]. Probably there are many who

[1] A good instance of this may be found in the article on
'Calendar' in the *Encyclopaedia Britannica*, an article which
has been reproduced from the 9th into the 11th edition un-
changed. The writers tell us that 'although it was not introduced at Rome till after the reign of Theodosius, it had been
employed from time immemorial in almost all Eastern countries;
and as it forms neither an aliquot part of the year nor of the
lunar month, those who reject the Mosaic recital will be at a
loss, as Delambre remarks, to assign to it an origin having much
semblance of probability.'

As I have seen the statement about Roman use reproduced
elsewhere, I may add that I know of no foundation for dating
the official introduction of the week at Rome so late as Theodosius' death (A.D. 395). There is a well-known decree of
Constantine (321) forbidding legal and commercial business,
though permitting necessary field labour, 'on the venerable

still think in this way, and I am far from wishing to speak contemptuously of them. But I cannot hold such a view myself, and my arguments are addressed to those who share my feelings.

I have felt it necessary to say something about these preliminary points, but I wish to make a very strong distinction between them and what follows. In the following sections I give for the most part the results of my own investigations or, perhaps I should say, of what I have verified. In what has just been said about the evidence or want of evidence for a primitive and widely diffused continuous week, I have necessarily had to retail at second-hand what I have gathered from modern writers, whose value and accuracy I have no means of judging—only oriental scholars can appraise them with any authority. But I am not disturbed by this; for even if later discoveries should shew that the week, whether in the planetary or any other form, was a primitive and general institution in the East, it would not affect my main purpose, which is to shew how the double conception involved in the Jewish and the planetary week took root in the Roman Empire and produced the institution under which we live. When the Graeco-Roman world adopted the seven-day week, it was not

day of the Sun' (*Codex Justiniani*, III, 12, 2): while an inscription from the Danube lands credits the same Emperor with a relaxation of this, so far as to permit 'nundinae' to be held on the Sun's day. (*Corp. Inscr. Lat.* III, 4121.)

because it was ancient, but because it embodied conceptions which had taken a remarkable hold over the popular mind.

Of these two factors which have produced our week, the Jewish is, at first sight at any rate, the more important. We measure our time in cycles of seven days primarily because the Jews, by the time of our era, had come to attach vast importance to the religious observance of one day in seven; because the first Christians were Jews; because, though Paul at any rate abjured the Sabbath for his Gentile converts, as strongly as he abjured circumcision, the Church still clung to the practice of meeting once every seven days; because thus the Christian Lord's day acquired something of the sanctity of the Sabbath, with which indeed so many people still confuse it; and finally because this religious institution has been found to have a civil value. But the planetary week of the pagan, in which not only one day is sacred, but each of the seven is held to be under the dominion of one or other of the seven bodies which 'wander' through the heavens, has been a contributory factor in various ways and the evidence of this is written unmistakably in the names of the days.

That our week-day names represent the planets may be regarded, I presume, as an accepted fact, though I have come across highly educated people, and indeed distinguished scholars, who were ignorant of it. It is indeed somewhat disguised if we take any language separately. The French *dimanche* and *samedi*[1], and more clearly the Italian *Domenica* and *Sabbato*, are ecclesiastical names for the Christian Lord's day and the Jewish Sabbath. But the other five correspond to the names which we still give to our own satellite and four of the planets in the modern use of the term. In Teutonic lands, on the other hand, these same four have been converted into Teutonic deities, whose names do not at first sight suggest a planetary origin, but the moon is there still, while Sunday and Saturday fill up the gap in the South-Europe languages. Thus between the Latin and the Teutonic we find Sun, Moon, Mars, Mercury, Jupiter, Venus, Saturn all represented. The evidence for the planetary character of the week does not stop here, as will be abundantly shewn in Section 3. But before dealing with this let us examine the history of the other factor, the Jewish week.

---

[1] Dialectically *sabedi*.

§ 2

THE JEWISH WEEK

The Jewish Sabbath, as we all know, was held by the Jews to go back to at least the time of Moses. Whatever we may think of the truth of this tradition, or of the date of the Decalogue in which the observance of the Sabbath is enjoined, it is certain that by the eighth century when Amos and Hosea wrote, it was a well-established institution. Both these prophets refer to it, Amos[1] as a day on which trading or bargaining was unlawful, Hosea[2] as one of the festivals of which the wrath of Jehovah would deprive Israel. In both these cases it is coupled with the New Moon, a point which may possibly have some significance as I have already noted. So too Isaiah[3] a little later makes Jehovah say that the Sabbaths and New Moons of degenerate Judah have become abominable in his sight. Jeremiah again, a century or more afterwards, speaks of the Sabbath as an ancestral, though often neglected, ordinance[4]. A later prophet, the author of Isaiah lvi and lviii, puts the obligation of the Sabbath still more emphatically. After the

[1] Am. viii, 5.   [2] Hos. iii, 4.   [3] Is. i, 13.
[4] Jer. xvii, 19–27, but the genuineness of this passage seems to be doubted.

return from the Captivity Nehemiah[1] shews all the horror of the later Jews at its profanation. Again it is well known that there are two versions of the Decalogue, one in Deuteronomy and the other in Exodus, and that while they both include the ordinance of the Sabbath they give different reasons for its observance. In Deuteronomy the commandment is based on the deliverance of Israel from Egypt, though the connexion is not clearly brought out[2]. In Exodus it is based on the belief that God having created the world in six days rested on the seventh[3], and this of course agrees with the narrative in the first chapter of the Bible. The dominant, if not the universal, opinion among scholars, at any rate at present, is that this narrative belongs to the later stratum of the Pentateuch, and those who hold this view will probably conclude that, while the ordinance was of immemorial antiquity in Israel, its origin had been forgotten. The only[4] point in extra-Biblical sources which has been thought by scholars to bear upon this question is one which has been already cursorily referred to, namely, that in the Babylonian records we find that the 7th, 14th, 19th[5], 21st and 28th days of the month, or at any

---

[1] Neh. xiii, 15 ff.   [2] Deut. v, 15.   [3] Ex. xx, 11.

[4] The controversies about the word 'schaputtu' have not, so far as I can judge as an outsider, any bearing on the subject.

[5] The intrusive 19th is usually explained as due to the fact that it would be 49th from the beginning of the preceding month.

rate of some months, were days on which certain
things were forbidden to the King[1]. But I will
not dwell on this partly because I have already
pointed out the vital difference between this
'lunar' week and the Jewish continuous week,
and also because we are not really concerned
with the origin[2] of the Jewish week or Sabbath,
but with the part which it has played in the
establishment of our own week.

To deal with this we must pass on to the time
of our own era. What the Jews themselves
thought of the Sabbath is most clearly shewn by
the Gospels and the picture which they present
of the indignation which our Lord's supposed
unorthodoxy roused among the Pharisees. But
it is more important to note that the ordinance
had attracted widespread interest and perhaps

[1] Some discussion of the bearing of these facts on the origin
of the Jewish Sabbath will be found in any recent article
or essay on the subject. My impression is that the tendency of
recent scholarship is to discount the reality of the connexion.

[2] It seems strange to me that Biblical scholars, who appear
to cling to the idea that the planetary week is of immemorial
antiquity, generally, I believe, reject the idea that the Hebrew
week was originally planetary. Their conclusion is quite agree-
able to me, since, as will appear, I do not believe in the early
origin of the planetary week. But if I saw reason to believe in
it, it would seem to me a very plausible hypothesis that the Sabbath began as an abstention from activity in view of the maleficent influence of Saturn and afterwards under Jehovism
received a different explanation. Amos v, 26 seems to be generally understood as an allusion to an early adoration of the planet
by Israel.

imitation in the nations among whom the Jews were dispersed. Josephus, in a treatise written to answer the attacks made upon the Jews by a scholar named Apion, says that there is no city, Greek or barbarian, nor any single nation 'in which the custom of abstention from work on the seventh day and other Jewish customs have not become a matter of common use.'[1] We may regard this statement as having some pardonable exaggeration, but it is confirmed to a considerable extent by more disinterested writers. Thus we find Seneca[2], when he wishes to give examples of superstitious ritual, mentioning the practice of 'lighting lamps on the Sabbath.' So too Juvenal[3], when he describes how the son of the 'Sabbath-fearer' and abstainer from pork becomes himself a complete Jew, sets it down as the fault of the father, who had kept every seventh day as a day of idleness. Here we seem to have two grades of Judaizers, the second a complete proselyte, the former observing the Sabbath and refusing to touch swine's flesh, but otherwise remaining an ordinary pagan. A few passages suggest a looser connexion than even this—that there were Romans, who felt no real attraction to Judaism, but still had some superstitious regard for the Sabbath. Ovid in his amatory exhortations three times couples the Sabbath with other days of leisure or inactivity.

[1] *Contra Apionem*, ii, 39 (40).
[2] *Epistles*, 95.   [3] *Satires*, xiv, 96

The lover may seek his mistress at the festivals
of Adonis or the 'Syrian Sabbath.'[1] If he wants
to escape her, he must not let himself be hindered
by the taboos which surround the ill-omened
anniversary of the Roman disaster on the Allia—
or the Sabbath[2]. Tibullus speaks in much the
same way in a passage to which I shall recur
more than once[3]. Every reader of Latin knows
Horace's famous satire of the bore whom he
tries to escape by enlisting the services of his
friend Fuscus[4]. 'You told me,' so runs the dialogue, 'that you wanted to have some private
talk with me.' Fuscus replies, 'Oh yes, but
some other time: today is the 30th Sabbath:
do you wish to scandalise the circumcised Jews?'
—'Oh, I have no scruple.'—'Yes, but I have:
I am a weak brother—one of the many: you
must excuse me—another time for our talk.'
And off goes Fuscus leaving Horace in the
clutches of the enemy. All this is perhaps not
to be taken too seriously. Fuscus in particular
talks, I believe, in sheer mischievousness[5], but
on the other hand, the irony would lose its point
if the educated Roman class, to which Horace
belonged, did not at least believe that the super-

---

[1] *Ars Amatoria*, I, 75, 415.
[2] *Remedia Amoris*, 219.   [3] *V. infra*, pp. 17, 35.
[4] Hor. *Sat.* I, 9, 67.
[5] And therefore the laborious attempts of commentators to
find a meaning for '30th sabbath' seem to me to be wasted.
Fuscus, or rather Horace, has just invented the phrase.

stition of the Sabbath was widespread among
less enlightened people.

A somewhat different form of evidence is
supplied by an incident related by Suetonius in
his Life of Tiberius[1]. Tiberius when living at
Rhodes wished to hear a certain Diogenes, a
'grammarian,' i.e. a literary lecturer. But
Diogenes only gave his public lectures on the
Sabbath, and when Tiberius asked for a special
reception, he merely received a message brought
by a slave that he must come on the seventh day.
Tiberius took the affront meekly, but later, when
he became Emperor, 'scored off' Diogenes,
when he wished to be admitted to his levée at
Rome, by telling him to come after seven years.
This curious form of Sabbath-keeping on Diogenes' part can hardly have been due to religious
feeling and I can only explain it on the supposition that there were so many people at leisure
on the Sabbath that he found it a suitable day to
collect an audience.

A further point of great significance must be
noted. We sometimes find the Sabbath spoken
of as 'Saturn's day.' Leaving out of consideration writers of the second or third century, we
have in the first century Frontinus[2], a writer on
military tactics, using this term, when he speaks
of the refusal of the Jews to fight on the Sabbath.
Tibullus[3], writing some time earlier than 18 B.C.

[1] Suet. *Tib.* 32.   [2] *Strategematon*, II, i, 17.
[3] Tib. *El.* I, 3, 18.

(the date of his death), when describing the reluctance which he had felt against undertaking a journey which ultimately turned out unluckily, says: 'I often alleged auguries and evil omens, or that I held the day of Saturn sacred.'[1] The parallel passages in Ovid leave little doubt that he means the Sabbath. Tacitus, in the famous though often nonsensical account of the Jews with which he prefaces his story of the fall of Jerusalem, gives as one theory of the Sabbath that it was held in honour of Saturn because 'of the seven stars which rule human affairs Saturn has the highest sphere and the chief power.'[2] Here we find the Jewish week linked on to the planetary, and I now pass on to an examination of the latter.

[1] Or 'accursed.'
[2] Tac. *Hist.* v, 4. We may add to these a passage in Dion Cassius, XLIX, 22, which though written in the third century probably comes from a much earlier authority. Describing a capture of Jerusalem about 38 B.C. he notes that this like the earlier one by Pompey (*v. infra*, p. 21) was effected on 'what was even then called Saturn's day.' Dion, as we shall see, was puzzled by the rise into common currency of the planetary week and very possibly he found this phrase in an earlier or perhaps contemporary authority and noted it as bearing on the question in which he was interested.

§ 3

THE PLANETARY WEEK

The conclusions to which I am led by the evidence given in this section may be summed up as follows. By the beginning of the third century A.D. the habit of measuring time in cycles of seven days, each of them dedicated to one of the seven planets, had become universal or at least general in private life throughout the Roman Empire, though it had not received official recognition. Evidence of the practice, though hardly proving a general adoption, can be traced back to at least A.D. 79. Passing over some doubtful testimonies, we find, as already stated, that a century before the last-mentioned date, the idea that the Sabbath was 'Saturn's day' had become current. Before this no trace of it can be found, and speculations as to its origin and antiquity must remain at the best mere speculations.

For a complete understanding of the evidence a preliminary explanation of one point is necessary. This is the order of the planets in the week. Now the normal arrangement of the planets according to their supposed distance from the Earth is as follows:

Moon, Mercury, Venus, Sun, Mars, Jupiter, Saturn.

This order, which, if we leave the Moon out of consideration, and put the Earth in the place of the Sun, is a correct order for the distance of the planets from the Sun and was based by the astronomers on their calculation of the time taken by each planet in its revolution, was the accepted order possibly from the days of Pythagoras and certainly from the second century B.C.[1] through the imperial period, the Dark Ages and the Middle Ages down to the establishment of Copernican astronomy. Thus, to take two examples from earlier and later times, we find it in Cicero's treatise on Divination in which he includes astrology[2]. And it forms the framework of Dante's *Paradiso*. Dante, as every reader will remember, ascends through seven zones beginning with the Moon and ending with Saturn, whence he passes into the eighth and ninth heavens known as the Primum Mobile and Empyrean which later astrology had added to the Seven.

On the other hand, the order of the planets in the week, as clearly reflected in the existing names, is:

Sun, Moon, Mars, Mercury, Jupiter, Venus, Saturn.

A full discussion of this difference between the

---

[1] *V. infra*, p. 58.
[2] Cic. *De Divinatione*, II, 91. In another treatise, the *De Natura Deorum*, II, 53, he makes Venus and Mercury change places.

two orders must be deferred, but we may here note that different as they are there is a definite relation between them. The week-order is obtained from the normal order by always *dropping two*. The moon is in the third place from the Sun—then if we go back to the top Mars is in the third place from the Moon, Mercury in the third place from Mars and so on till we finally get back to the Sun. Now the importance of this for our present purpose lies in the fact that when we find the Seven arranged in week-order instead of normal order, we may be fairly sure that those who thus arranged them knew and observed the planetary week.

This being made clear, we may pass on to the evidence[1]. It will be convenient to start from the point when we know the planetary week to have come into general use and then working backwards to see how much earlier we can trace it. This point is found in a passage[2] of Dion Cassius, an eminent and careful historian, who

---

[1] Most of the examples given in the next few pages will be found in an article by Schürer in the *Zeitschrift für die Neutestamentliche Wissenschaft,* 1905, entitled 'Die siebentägige Woche im Gebrauche der Christlichen Kirche der ersten Jahrhunderte.' The title is misleading in a sense, for the article contains a vast amount of facts and references bearing on the week in general. In fact its only inadequacy is that Schürer was not acquainted with the astrological documents edited by Kroll. I should add that I have accepted Schürer's statements with regard to coins, wall paintings and the like. All literary and inscriptional references have been verified.

[2] xxxvii, 18.

wrote the history of Rome from the earliest date
to his own time. The history was actually carried
up to the year A.D. 229, but various remarks
shew that the first part is to be dated earlier, and
we may fairly place the passage which now concerns us somewhere between the years 210 and
220. In his 37th book (the total number is 80,
the majority of which are lost or exist only in
abridgments), he has come to the capture of
Jerusalem by Pompey in 63 B.C. and notes that
this would never have been accomplished but for
the Jews' reverence for 'Saturn's day.' Not only
as this came round did they allow the Romans to
continue their siege operations unhindered, but
the final assault was also made on a 'Saturn's
day' and met with no resistance. He then proceeds to give some account of the Jews and in
particular how 'they have consecrated the so-
called day of Saturn and while performing on
it many observances peculiar to themselves lay
their hands to no serious work.' The passage
then goes on as follows:

And as for Saturn, his personality, the source of the
honours thus paid to him and the nature of the superstitious awe shewn to him have been treated by many
writers and have no connexion with this history. But
the dedication of the days to the stars called planets
originated in Egypt, but is now universal though its
origin is comparatively recent. Certainly the old Greeks,
to the best of my knowledge, knew nothing about it.
But since now it is an established usage among the Roman
as well as all other nations, and indeed may be called an

accepted tradition with them in a sense, I wish to give some little discussion of the method of arrangement of the days.

Dion then proceeds to suggest explanations of the remarkable order of the planets in the week, and these I will give when we come to deal with that point. Meanwhile the passage so far contains three statements, (1) the planetary week originated in Egypt, (2) it is of recent growth, (3) it was in his time in general, indeed universal, use. Of these statements the first perhaps cannot be accepted as certain. The original source of a usage which spread so silently, as the week seems to have spread, is not an easy matter to determine for a modern and still less for an ancient observer. The second is couched in too vague language to be of much value. But the universality of the practice in his own time is a matter on which we may accept his authority as decisive, even if it were not confirmed, as it is, by contemporary evidence.

Of this evidence the most interesting item is a passage in Philostratus' Life of Apollonius of Tyana[1], which is probably of almost exactly the same date as the part of Dion's history from which I have quoted. Philostratus was one of the greatest of the rhetoricians (a term which covers more or less our essayists, lecturers and preachers) of the third century. His most note-worthy work is this biography of Apollonius,

[1] III, 41.

a remarkable person, partly philosopher and
partly charlatan of the first century. Philostratus relates how when Apollonius was travel-
ling in India he received from Iarchas the chief
of the Brahmins seven rings bearing the names
of the seven planets, which he wore 'according
to the names of the days.' Clearly this refers to
the planetary week. Now Philostratus professes
to derive this statement that his hero had a ring
for every day of the week from a disciple or
companion of Apollonius called Damis, whose
memoirs had fallen into his hands. Whether
there really was such a book, or if there was,
whether it was really written by a companion of
Apollonius has always been a moot question.
If we take the story at its face value, since Apollonius' visit to India is supposed to be dated
somewhere between A.D. 40 and 60 it would
shew that some observance of a planetary week
existed at that time. But this is not of real importance for my present purpose. We shall find
other undoubtedly contemporary evidence that
the planetary week was recognized by some
people in the first century, and if so, it was only
to be expected, indeed it might almost be taken
for granted, that Apollonius, who had a strong
leaning to the occult and was credited with a
work on astrology, should have known and used
it. The value of the passage lies in its wording.
Philostratus wrote for the general reader. In
fact his work has often been thought to be a

counter blast to the Gospels. When he speaks
of Apollonius wearing his planetary rings 'according to the names of the days,' it is clearly
assumed that the general public knows without
further explanation that every day in a cycle of
seven was named after a planet.

Another valuable witness is found or supposed to be found in a little Greek and Latin
text book on grammar ascribed to one Dositheus
and dated in A.D. 207, where we find a list of the
days of the seven planets with the Latin and
Greek names in the order Saturn, Sun, Moon,
Mars, Mercury, Jupiter, Venus[1]. Incidentally
we observe that here we find the week beginning
with Saturday, an idea which the next section
will shew to be reasonable and natural. But a
more important inference is that, as the grammar
was no doubt intended for school uses we find
that in the beginning of the third century, chil-
dren had to learn the names of the week-days,
much as I remember to have recited in childhood:

Thirty days have September, April, June and
November, etc.

And at the same time it suggests to us that,
though the week is in such general use that it
has to be known, it is not so familiar that every-

---

[1] *Corpus Glossariorum Latinorum*, ed. Goetz, III, p. 58.
But I think this testimony must be received with some caution.
I am not sure that the date which is given as 'the consulship of
Maximus and Aper' applies to the whole of the contents.

one is sure to know it without formally learning
it. I never heard of school-children to-day being
taught the names of the week-days. And this
again is natural enough, for while our civil life
is regulated by the week, it is, as we shall see,
the most remarkable fact about the planetary
week that it spread without any civil or official
recognition—that nothing happened in it, as
things happen to us on Sunday.

Further we may note that an inscription belonging to A.D. 205 has been found in Karlsburg
in Transylvania, where the date is given not only
by the year and the month, but also by the week-
day, in this case Monday[1]. Another, not quite
so complete, but probably belonging to A.D. 231,
comes from Kelheim in Bavaria, while represen-
tations of the Seven in week-order some of which
at least are ascribed by experts to this period
have been found in the Rhineland[2]. All these
go to shew that Dion's statement applies not
only to the centre of the empire, but to its most
outlying parts.

Finally, before we leave the early decades of
the third century, we may listen to the witness
of the Christian Church. Tertullian, writing
about or possibly before A.D. 200, in two very
similar passages scoffs at the pagan week[3]. The
details of these passages, as so often with this
most difficult of writers, are obscure. But the

---

[1] *V.* Schürer, p. 33.   [2] *Ib.*

[3] *Apologeticum,* 16; *Ad nationes,* 1, 13.

general sense is something like this. Pagans
often say that the Christians worship the sun.
They think this partly from our custom of turn-
ing to the east and partly because we hold a
festival on the Sun's day. But our religion is not
sun-worship and if we rejoice on the Sun's day
we do but follow the pagans, who dedicate the
day which precedes it, Saturn's day, to leisure
and feasting. Here we seem to have the suggestion that the day of the sinister planet had
first, because of its unluckiness, been held to be
unsuitable for active work and then by a natural
transformation had become a festival or holiday.
We have seen much the same thing happen with
the old Scottish Fast-days and our own Good
Friday.

That the planetary week was a matter of
common knowledge and observance *after* Dion's
day is attested by a great body of inscriptional
and other evidence. But I need not weary the
reader with the details, for the truth of the statement is shewn most effectively by the simple
fact that in spite of the opposition of the Church
the planetary names held their ground in the
Christianized empire at any rate in the West[1].
It is true that where ecclesiastical names were
available they could prevail. As already noticed,
'Dominica' and 'Sabbatum' ousted Sun's day and

---

[1] The Eastern Church seems to have been much more suc-
cessful. The names of the days both in Modern Greek and
Russian are not planetary; *v.* Appendix, pp. 117 ff.

Saturn's day over most of Southern Europe. But
the plain numbers for the 2nd, 3rd, 4th and 5th
days, though regularly used by orthodox Church
writers, took no popular root[1]. Our task is to
find how far *before* Dion's time we can trace the
planetary week. The first writer as we move
backwards through the second century is
Clement of Alexandria, one of the greatest and
most liberal-minded of the Fathers. The Christian fast-days he observes[2] are the fourth day and
the 'preparation,' i.e. Wednesday and Friday,
and in this the enlightened will see an allegory.
For these days are named after Mercury and
Venus, and in fasting on them we symbolize the
larger truth that our whole lives must be a fast
from avarice (Mercury) and lust (Venus). This
utilization of a piece of paganism to point a
Christian moral is entirely after Clement's manner and we must not draw from his words an
inference, which would be contradicted by
plentiful evidence, that devout or strict Christians were reconciled to the use of the planetary names. But his words do shew that the
planetary week was an accepted usage of the
pagan world, in which the Christian necessarily
moved.

We next come to a famous passage in the
Apology of Justin Martyr[3]. This defence of

---

[1] Portugal is an exception; *v.* App. p. 118.
[2] *Stromateis*, VII, 12 (p. 877, Potter).
[3] *Ap.* I, 67.

Christian doctrine and practice addressed to the
Emperor Antoninus Pius and his adopted sons
about A.D. 150 has a chapter in which the Christian weekly meeting is described. The whole
chapter has an immense importance for the
student of Christian antiquities, but I need only
quote a small part of it. 'It is on what is called
the Sun's day that all who abide in the town or
the country come together,' (here follows an
account of the reading of the Gospels at the
meeting and the celebration of the Eucharist),
'and we meet on the Sun's day because it is the
first day on which God formed darkness and
mere matter into the world and Jesus Christ,
our saviour, rose from the dead. For on the day
before Saturn's day they crucified him, and on
the day after Saturn's day which is the Sun's
day he appeared to his apostles and disciples and
taught them the things which I have transmitted
for your examination.' Two points in this passage may be noted. First Justin assumes that
two of the planetary names, Saturn's day and
Sun's day, will be known to the Emperors, but
he does not mention by name the day of Venus.
It has been suggested that he does not wish to
sully his page with the name of the adulterous
goddess; I cannot think that this is at all likely.
Saturn also is the hero of discreditable stories
which Christian fathers were not slow to satirize.
I have been inclined to suggest that Justin was
hazy about the week-names, or at any rate

thought that the Emperor might not be familiar
with them all. The Sun's day is mentioned by
name, because it is the day with which the
chapter is concerned. The mention of Friday is
merely incidental and therefore the Emperor
need not be troubled with its special name. If
this is right, we might infer that the planetary
week was not so well established in popular
usage and knowledge as it was when Dion wrote
60 years later, though on the other hand we
must not make too much of a perhaps accidental
omission. The other point is the position which
Saturday holds in Justin's scheme. That day too
comes in only incidentally, even more so than
Friday, for nothing is mentioned as happening
on it. But it is evidently the pivot on which the
week turns, the day from which the others are
measured. For the present I only note this in
passing. I shall recur to it, when we come to
deal with the relations between the Jewish and
the planetary week.

Another, but to my mind, doubtful, piece of
evidence in the earliest part of the second century is connected with the Emperor Trajan
(98–117). A biographer of the fourth century,
Lampridius[1], notes that Alexander Severus,
Emperor from 222 to 235, made certain res-
torations or changes in the public baths. One

[1] *Scriptores Historiae Augustae*, xviii, 25. The text is in
part corrupt, but there can be little doubt about the general
meaning.

of them was that he named a basin after Oceanus, whereas Trajan 'had dedicated the basins to the Days.' Presumably by this he means the seven deities of the week. If we took the statement as it stands, it would be of some importance. The most mysterious fact about the spread of week-observance is that it was apparently accomplished without official recognition, and here we might seem to have some semblance of official recognition. But I fear it cannot be relied on. By Lampridius' time the planetary week was universal and if Trajan had recognized the seven planets or planetary gods Lampridius would naturally suppose that this involved recognition of the week-days over which in his time they presided. But this is not necessarily the case. It is all-important to remember that reverence for the great Seven does not involve the idea that time is measured by them. The implication in Lampridius' statement could only be proved if we knew that Trajan arranged the basins, which no doubt were distinguished by planetary statues or symbols, in week-order instead of normal order, and this we do not know.

When we add to these a coin of the time of Antoninus Pius found in Egypt and bearing, among other figures, seven, which are *supposed* to represent the seven planets in week-order[1], we shall, I believe, have exhausted the evidence which may with any certainty be assigned to the

[1] *Vide* Schürer, p. 23.

second century[1]. We may now pass on to the
first, and here we have the testimony of no less a
name than Plutarch[2]. In the great body of his
philosophical and general works which usually
go under the name of *Moralia*, works which,
though they have not exercised on posterity the
same influence as the famous *Lives*, are a
treasury of information on the culture and religion of his time, there is a set of essays in the
form of dialogues called *Symposia* or Table-talk.

[1] Among the monumental and inscriptional evidence there
is probably a certain amount or perhaps much which *may* belong
to this century or even to the preceding one. The only literary
point known to me and not included above is to be found in
one Ampelius, whose *Liber Memorialis*, though it does not
mention the week, in describing the planets puts them in week-
order. There are strong reasons for placing Ampelius in the
second century, but this early date is not universally accepted.

I should perhaps also mention an 'oracle' adduced by
Porphyry the celebrated Neoplatonist and quoted from him by
Eusebius (*Praeparatio Evangelica*, v, 14, 1). This oracle, which
is in a fragmentary form and as it stands partly corrupt, probably
named the seven planet-gods, though not in week-order, and
bade the worshipper invoke them. It certainly (and this is the
point which concerns us) bade him invoke the Sun on the Sun's
day and the Moon on the Moon's day. Porphyry wrote somewhere in the second half of the third century, but it is a fair
supposition that the oracle dates from a considerably earlier
time. It may probably therefore belong to the second century
and may quite conceivably be as early as any evidence of the
planetary week. But the matter is too uncertain for any stress
to be laid upon it.

[2] *Sympos.* iv, 7. The greater part of Plutarch's life belongs
to the first century, but possibly this work may date from the
earliest years of the second.

One of these bears the title 'Why are the days
named after the planets reckoned in a different
order from the actual order?' By an unlucky
chance only the title of this particular dialogue
has survived, but this title shews the subject unmistakably. Still more important are some facts
revealed by the discoveries at Pompeii[1]. It is
hardly necessary to point out that testimony from
Pompeii has the merit that one limit of its date
is fixed beyond dispute. It may be much earlier
than the destruction of the city in A.D. 79 but it
cannot be later. The clearest item is a wall-
inscription in Greek headed 'Days of the Gods'
followed by a list of the Seven in week-order beginning with Saturn and ending with Venus.
Another wall-inscription (this time in Latin) has
no heading and Mercury's name is omitted[2], but
the remaining six are in week-order, while two
others mention the 'Sun's day' and the 'Moon's
day.'[3] There is also a fresco in which appear
figures clearly representing the seven deities in
week-order.

From this point the evidence becomes somewhat uncertain. One passage, which is often
pressed into service, comes from the fragmentary *Satyricon* of Petronius, which may be dated

[1] *V*. Schürer, pp. 27, 28.
[2] Have we in these two cases attempts of schoolboys to
memorize the days of the week, after the manner of Dositheus'
pupils, but in the second with less success?
[3] One of these is definitely dated as A.D. 60.

about A.D. 60[1]. By far the best known episode
in this earliest of novels is the story of the evening
spent in feasting at the house of the rich but
vulgar parvenu Trimalchio in Naples. On one of
Trimalchio's doorposts was fixed a tablet 'shewing the courses of the Moon and paintings of the
Seven Stars and different marks to shew what
days were lucky and what unlucky.' Here the
'Seven Stars' are clearly the seven planets, but
it is not stated that they were in week-order.
The only suggestion of a week comes in the
words 'what days were lucky or unlucky,' and
this may quite well refer to the days of the month.
Even if we insist on connecting them with the
'Seven Stars,' they may be astrological in the
proper sense and refer to the various combinations or positions of the planets on particular
days. We know that calendars of this kind
existed and were used even by astrologically-
minded doctors in dieting their patients. And if
it be objected that it would be difficult to
represent these in a single tablet on Trimalchio's
door, we have to remember the licence of the
novelist who did not have to construct the tablet
in actual fact. If the words are taken, as is no
doubt quite possible, of the week, we may see
in them a confirmation of the view which on
other grounds seems probable that it was among
the vulgar rather than the educated that the
week originally obtained its currency.

[1] *Sat.* 30.

Another doubtful item belongs to a considerably earlier date. This is the fragment of a calendar which experts consider to belong to a few years before or after our era[1]. I have already stated that Roman calendars marked the periodical recurrence of the nundinae or market days on every eighth day by the letters *a* to *h*. This calendar is an exception or rather a partial exception, for the days are marked from *a* to *h* in one column, but *a* to *g* in another. Here undoubtedly we have a seven-day week and it may quite possibly be the planetary week, though no planetary names are attached. But there are other possibilities. I do not think we can altogether rule out the suggestion that since this fragment was found in Sabine territory, the second column marks a local variety of the 'nundinatio' by which these market-days were held every seventh instead of every eighth day[2]. That local needs might make such a variation desirable is *prima facie* possible enough. Again it is possible that it was intended for Jews. For the presence and influence of the Jews in Italy in the time of Augustus is certainly quite as marked as the influence of the astrologers[3].

[1] *V*. Schürer, p. 26.

[2] This view is adopted by Marquardt, *loc. cit.* (*v.* p. 3).

[3] Another probable employment of the seven-day week for calendar purposes, in the first century A.D. (this time with almost certainly the planetary names in week-order), appears in a fragment, which seems intended to mark the market-days in various towns of central Italy. A representation and

Finally, some few years probably before this we have the passage from Tibullus already mentioned, 'I alleged that I held the day of Saturn sacred.' That Tibullus is primarily alluding to the Sabbath seems to me, as I have said, almost certain. But does he in calling it 'Saturn's day' shew a knowledge of the planetary week? It seems to me the most natural conclusion that he does, but I do not think it is absolutely certain. The belief that the Sabbath was a Jewish form of reverencing the planet *may* have originated independently of the planetary week and indeed be anterior to it. That Saturn was an unlucky planet is a doctrine independent of the week and we may safely suppose that before the week came into use there were what we may call 'real' Saturn's days when the planet was actually in a position which the astrologers reckoned as unfavourable to enterprise. Then the Gentile world observing the Jewish abstention from work and misreading the day of rest and rejoicing as a day of superstitious dread of activity may have evolved the theory of its connexion with Saturn.

At any rate with Tibullus our knowledge of the planetary week comes to an end[1]. Nothing

attempted restoration is given in *Corp. Lat. Inscript.* I, p. 218, but I cannot pretend to understand it fully.

[1] A passage in Horace (*Sat.* II, 3, 291) sometimes quoted as evidence of week-observance would be about the same date as Tibullus. I regard this interpretation of the line as very forced and unnatural, but as it has been accepted by respectable authorities, I have discussed it in Appendix, pp. 124 f.

that can with any probability be construed as involving or alluding to it has been discovered at any earlier date. That at the time when we first hear of it, whether we fix that time by the discoveries at Pompeii or the words of Tibullus, it was a comparative innovation in the Graeco-Roman world may be safely inferred from what we know of the literature and history of that world. Whether it had long existed elsewhere is, as I have said before, a matter of mere speculation, though a few remarks suggesting the contrary will be offered later. Meanwhile, reviewing the evidence discussed above, we see that the planetary week was known in some sense in the Empire as early as the destruction of Pompeii and most people will think a century earlier. But it should not be inferred that it was then known in the same sense as in Dion's time. The evidence, as we trace it backwards, tapers downward not only in quantity, but in quality. Justin is perhaps the earliest writer who assumes that the casual reader will understand the week without explanation: Plutarch was a researcher into out-of-the-way cults and might quite well discuss a subject which was only known to the astrologically-minded. Even the remains of Pompeii hardly shew popular usage. People who cherish beliefs which are not held or understood by their neighbours may embody them in inscriptions or frescoes for their own pleasure or edification. The evidence, in fact, if it does not actually support, is quite compatible with the natural view that knowledge of the week spread gradually through the Empire till it reached the universality expressed in Dion's words. We can easily imagine various stages in this from our own experience. Fifty years ago, I suppose, the feast of Corpus Christi was known only to Roman Catholics. To-day a great many Anglo-Catholics observe it and consequently it is known to a wider circle, who, however, would for the most part be puzzled to say how and when in the year it is fixed. To take a stage above this, probably most Scottish Presbyterians know that there is such a day as Ascension Day, but I should be surprised if the majority could locate it, or even know that it always comes on a Thursday. If the circle which observes either of these days should through some wave of feeling widen greatly, if for instance schools had to be closed, because so many of the pupils were required to treat them as days of religious observance, the general public would soon come to know their incidence, as well as it now knows Christmas or Easter Monday. Some such process as this we may suppose to have gone on in the Empire in the first two centuries under the stress of an increasing volume of popular belief and feeling.

What the nature of this belief was we shall have to enquire later. Meanwhile we may note that the most remarkable fact about the evidence we have reviewed is its meagre and casual nature.

The casualness is in itself a testimony to its genuineness. It is not of a kind which could be invented or imagined. But at the same time it suggests strongly that the movement to week-observance was in a sense sub-conscious, that it was a movement of the masses and not of the educated. In this respect it stands in contrast to Judaism and official astrology, both of which had their adherents in high places and were matters of interest to the classes, from which our extant literature springs.

THE RELATION OF THE JEWISH TO THE PLANETARY WEEK. CHRONOCRATORIES OR 'TIME SOVEREIGNTIES' OF THE PLANETS

In the second section it was shewn that the Jewish Sabbath had in the early years of our era obtained a curiously strong hold over a considerable portion of the population of the Empire and in particular that a belief had sprung up in some quarters that this Sabbath was in reality a 'Saturn's day,' in other words that the abstention from work practised thereon by the Jews was caused by their wish to avoid the influence of the dangerous planet Saturn. Two very different inferences might be plausibly drawn from these facts.

On the one hand it might be held that the popular reverence for the Sabbath was based entirely on this misconception and was nothing but a reverence for Saturn's day. The multitude, obsessed by the belief that the planets ruled on successive days, interpreted the Jewish observance in this sense, and called it Sabbath or Saturn's day very much at random. In this case the planetary feeling is the dominant factor and its coincidence with the Jewish observance is merely incidental.

On the other hand it may be suggested that the Jewish Sabbath is at the bottom of the whole

thing. The Graeco-Roman world, it might be
held, all agog for Oriental imported cults, seized
upon Sabbath-keeping as one of especial note
and having further somehow imbibed the belief that it was concerned with the planet Saturn,
proceeded to build upon it a planetary system.
Indeed it was fairly obvious that if a day consecrated to Saturn recurred every seventh day,
the six intervening days would be assigned to
the other six planets. Once constructed the
theory would soon forget its Jewish origin and
hold the world captive on its merits. This view,
of course, assumes a comparatively late origin
for the planetary week.

Neither of these views is to my mind satisfactory or on examination tenable, though both,
particularly the second, may contain an element
of truth.

My objection to the first rests on the fact that
the allusions to the Sabbath, especially in the
first century, are far more abundant than the
allusions either to the planetary week as a whole
or to Saturn's day in particular. The way in
which Horace, Ovid, Seneca and later Juvenal
and many other writers speak of the Jewish
observance shews that in spite of certain miscon-
ceptions they thought of it as a definitely Jewish
practice, not as a mere variation of a pagan superstition. Tibullus' words on one interpretation,
as well as the other passages where the Sabbath
is called Saturn's day with undoubted reference

to the planetary week, can be set on the other side, but they are few in comparison. At the same time, there is, as I have said, a certain element of truth in this view. I have little doubt that the existence of the planetary week and the fact that the day on which the Jew abstained from work coincided with the day of the planet most adverse to enterprise promoted Sabbatarianism, and served to confirm many outsiders in the belief that it and Judaism in general deserved their respect and imitation.

The other view that the Jewish Sabbath was the parent of the planetary week cannot be set aside on merely chronological grounds, and it has this much on its side, that while the passages which bring the Sabbath and the planetary week into connexion with each other are a small proportion of those which speak of the Sabbath, they are a very large proportion of those which speak of the week. In fact, it may be said that, if we leave inscriptions and the like out of the question, a considerable majority of the literary allusions to the week are introduced by a mention of the Sabbath. This is the case with Tibullus (again adopting the usual interpretation of his words) and Frontinus[1]. It is the case with Justin, and I have already noted that with him the Sabbath or Saturn's day is the pivot of the week, and that from it the other days are measured. It is the case with the great passage in Dion Cassius.

[1] *V*. p. 16.

It may very possibly be also the case with Plutarch, for it is significant that his lost dialogue on the order of the planets in the week follows immediately on two others on 'Why the Jews refuse to eat pork,' and 'What is the God of the Jews?' We may fairly assume that, if planetary devotion, as I suggested above, often led to Sabbatarianism, it is still more true that the latter gave support or something more to the former. And I should be inclined to go further and suspect that among the more educated classes the Sabbath was for long a more familiar idea than the planetary week and that they regarded the latter as a semi-Jewish business. It is only by looking at that keystone of the whole subject, the ORDER of the days, that we can assure ourselves that the planetary week had a quite independent origin. If it were nothing more than a pagan interpretation of the Jewish week, which assumed that the Sabbath was Saturn's day and then proceeded to fill up the other six, we should presumably find the planets in their normal order which, we should remember, was believed to be their real order. We should expect that the series would either adopt the Jewish view that Saturn ended the week and culminate with that planet or else ignoring this take Saturn's day as the first and work downwards. In the first case we should get a week running:

Moon, Mercury, Venus, Sun, Mars, Jupiter, Saturn.

In the second case the reverse of this. As we all know, we get something quite different from either, and here at last we must deal fully with this vital question, why the week-order of the planets is what it is.

The quotation from Dion Cassius, the first part of which was given on page 21, proceeds as follows:

I have heard two explanations given of the order... The first is as follows. Apply the harmony called Diapason which holds the supremacy in music to these stars among which the sphere of heaven is parted out, following the order in which they severally make their revolutions. Begin with the outermost circle which is ascribed to Saturn; pass over the two next and set down the name of the deity which presides over the fourth circle. Again pass over two more thus reaching the seventh: go in this same way round and round the circles and their presiding deities. Apply the names thus obtained to the days and you will find that on this musical principle they agree with the arrangement in which the heaven is ordered.

This explanation need not detain us. In fact, I doubt whether it is an explanation at all or anything more than a statement of the fact we have already noted that the week-order is obtained from the normal order of the planets *by dropping two each time*, with the addition that in this it follows the analogy of the Diapason. I pass on to his second explanation:

The second explanation is as follows. Reckon the hours of the day and night; assign the first to Saturn,

the second to Jupiter, the third to Mars, the fourth to
the Sun, the fifth to Venus, the sixth to Mercury, and
the seventh to the Moon in the order accepted by the
Egyptians. Repeat this process and when you have gone
through the 24 hours you will find that the first hour
of the second day belongs to the Sun. Again repeat the
process throughout the second day or Sun's day and you
will assign the first hour of the third day to the Moon.
Go through the other days in the same way and each
day will obtain the deity with which it is connected.

As it is all-important to grasp the meaning of
this, I will risk incurring the charge of unnecessary repetition. If each hour in succession is
assigned to a planet, taking them in the normal
order, the 8th, the 15th and the 22nd will fall
to the planet with which we begin. The 23rd
will therefore belong to the 2nd planet on our
list, the 24th to the 3rd, and the 1st of the next
day to the 4th, so that, as we have seen is the
case, to find the planet which begins the next
day, we have always to drop two from that which
began the day before. I append a diagram for
two of the days.

SATURDAY (hours)

Saturn	1st–8th–15th–22nd
Jupiter	2nd–9th–16th–23rd
Mars	3rd–10th–17th–24th
Sun	4th–11th–18th
Venus	5th–12th–19th
Mercury	6th–13th–20th
Moon	7th–14th–21st

(Thus the 25th, i.e. the 1st of the next day, belongs to
the Sun.)

SUNDAY (hours)

Saturn	5th–12th–19th
Jupiter	6th–13th–20th
Mars	7th–14th–21st
Sun	1st–8th–15th–22nd
Venus	2nd–9th–16th–23rd
Mercury	3rd–10th–17th–24th
Moon	4th–11th–18th

(Thus the 25th, i.e. the 1st of the next day, belongs to
the Moon.)

Now I feel little or no doubt that this explanation is the right one, though it is true that
earlier authorities have questioned it or suggested other explanations. Jensen[1], for instance,
suggested that the week-order was determined
by the metals and colours associated with the
planets. Gold, he says, belonged to the Sun,
silver to the Moon. These are the most valuable
metals and come first. Of the colours red, the
most highly esteemed, belongs to Mars, black,
the least esteemed, to Saturn. This determined
their place in the week-order. What the three
intervening colours were he does not state. But
Jensen does not seem to have known what to my
mind is the overwhelming reason for accepting
Dion's second explanation, namely, that it was

[1] *V. Zeitschrift für Deutsche Wortforschung*, 1901, p. 157.
For full discussion of the earlier theories put forward notably
by Scaliger (it is only right to add that this prince of scholars
was well acquainted with Dion Cassius' explanations and re-
jected them) *v.* Hare in the article mentioned in the preface.

on this theory that the astrological world based
its practice. If we look through the seven volumes of Kroll's *Catalogue of the Codices of Greek
Astrologers*, enumerating many hundreds of
treatises, we shall find not unfrequently titles and
occasionally more or less complete documents,
which shew clearly that the week is mapped out
in 168 hours, with different influences ascribed
to them. The details, many of which are exceedingly fantastic, will be better left till we enquire what the week meant in fact for the general
public, which so universally adopted it. But the
general theory evidently is that while every hour
is attributed to a planet, which is called its 'controller,'[1] the whole day is under the 'regent,'[2]
which controls its first hour. These two influences modify each other. In the 1st, 8th,
15th and 22nd hours of any given day the
'regent' and 'controller' are identical: in the
others they are different. Thus to take 'Saturn's
day' with which the series begins, in the four
hours mentioned, the unlucky planet will be the
sole influence and all our actions will be liable
to misfortune. Jupiter and Venus, on the other
hand, are beneficent, so these same hours on
Thursday and Friday will be fortunate. But let
us take the 2nd, 9th, 16th and 23rd on Saturday,
or the 7th, 14th, 21st on Thursday. In the first
case we have Saturn as 'regent' and Jupiter as
'controller': in the second case the reverse of

[1] διέπων.   [2] πολεύων.

this. The two planets will more or less neutralize each other, though, as the functions of 'regent' and 'controller' are not quite the same, the resultants will not be quite identical. In fact, in each day fate will have seven different possibilities for us, and as no day has the same regent as another, it follows that we shall have to master 49 different combinations of influences before we can regulate our weekly days with safety.

Of these astrologers the most valuable witness is one Vettius Valens, whose work has been edited in full by Kroll. His importance lies in the fact that he may most probably be dated as early as the middle of the second century A.D. This is to be inferred from the period within which he sets the dates which he takes as examples for astrological calculations. For instance, in his chapter on the week[1], he gives directions by which a person knowing the year and month and day of his birth may calculate on what day of the week it fell. The example he gives is what would be in our calendar 7th Feb. A.D. 119, and no date used in this way is later than 158[2]. Valens has exactly the same doctrine as described above about the 'regent' and the 'controller' of days and hours with an extension to the month

[1] p. 26, Kroll's edition.
[2] On p. 33, there is an enumeration of the years of each Emperor down to Philippus, A.D. 248. But this passage is only found in one MS, and is regarded by Kroll as spurious (Pref. p. vi).

and the year, which I shall have to discuss presently. Meanwhile it is worth noting that this hour-lore, though I do not believe it had any deep root in the popular imagination, lived on to the Middle Ages and was known to Chaucer. The scheme which regulates the hours and days of the week is given in detail in his *Astrolabe*. But its most striking appearance is in the *Knight's Tale*[1]. Palamon on Sunday night goes to pray in the temple of Venus 'at her hour,' which we are expressly told is two hours before sunrise, the day being still astrologically measured from sunrise to sunrise. In the third hour from this at sunrise Emily prays in the temple of Diana or the Moon, and Arcite visits Mars' temple at Mars' next hour from this. It will be easily seen that this quite agrees with the scheme. The 23rd hour of Sunday belongs to Venus; the first hour of the next day, Monday at sunrise, belongs to the Moon; and Arcite's hour of prayer was the fourth of Monday. It may be added that Palamon, who put himself under the guardianship of the beneficent Venus, is very appropriately victorious over the votary of the sinister Mars[2].

Valens as I said above extends this system of

[1] Lines 2217, 2273, 2367.
[2] I have also come across the theory of the planetary hours in Roger Bacon's *Computus* (ch. 11) (a century or so before Chaucer). I have no doubt that research would discover many links between them and the early astrologers.

'regent' and 'controller' to other measures of time. As the planet of the first hour determines the planet of the day, so that of the first hour (and therefore the first day) of the month determines that of the month and so again with the year. In 1926 we open with a Friday. Venus is therefore regent of the year and also of the months of January and October. In the 1st, 8th, 15th and 22nd hours of the same and the 29th days of these months she is regent of hour, day, month and year, but only then. All through the rest of the year her sway is disputed by one, two or three planets. So Valens assures us, though he gives us no hints as to how we are to comport ourselves in the face of this plurality and indeed multitude of sovereigns. For there seems to be no reason why we should stop at the year and not provide a regent for the lustre, the decade, the century and the millennium. Even in the limited form in which Valens puts it, the thought is appalling; and it is no wonder that the popular imagination stopped short at the day and seems to have known little or nothing of regents of the month and year.

We now see the week in a somewhat different light. In the first place its unit is the hour not the day. In the second place, it is a link in a larger system of what are called 'chronocratories' or 'time sovereignties' of the planets. This extension of popular rather than scientific astrology deserves some consideration.

In scientific astrology—if I may be allowed to
use such an epithet at all of such a pseudo-
science—the influence of the planets is de-
pendent on their relations to one another and
the fixed stars. But the more popular view of
astrology, having learnt to conceive of the Seven
as the interpreters if not the lords of fate,
naturally extended their powers to provinces
with which their actual movements had nothing
to do. Thus various countries were supposed to
be under the domination of particular planets.
So too with plants, animals and metals, and this
last idea still survives in the name of Mercury
given to quicksilver. When the idea is extended
to time its most rational, or, at any rate, its least
irrational application is to the stages of human
life. That the seven ages of man should be
thought to be each under the dominion of a
planet was unavoidable. Thus we have Ptolemy's
scheme (though it does not appear to be the only
one) by which infancy is assigned to the Moon
up to four years old, childhood to Mercury till
14, adolescence to Venus till 22, youth to the
Sun till 41, full manhood to Mars till 56, early
old age to Jupiter till 68, after which comes the
reign of Saturn. This scheme, it will be observed,
like our own chronocratory of the week in its
original hour-form, follows the normal order of
the planets, the only difference being that it goes
up from the Moon to Saturn, instead of down
from Saturn to the Moon.

When this idea of planet sovereignty is applied to time in general, it obviously labours under one difficulty from which the other varieties which I have mentioned are free. In the case of plants, animals or metals, when we have once made up our mind which belongs to which planet, our difficulties are at an end. Saturn presides over onions, donkeys and lead, we are told. Well and good! We know these objects when we see them and can act upon our knowledge. So too with the 'chronocratory' of human life. We all know when we reach the age of 68 and pass from the presidency of Jupiter to that of Saturn. But how are we to know what day or hour belongs to each planet? True, when the sequence is once under way, we can follow it automatically. Sunday follows Saturday and Monday Sunday to all eternity. But what starting-point had it, as the chronocratory of human life has the birth for its starting-point? On the assumption that the planetary week has come down unbroken from some remote or prehistoric antiquity, we could only answer that we cannot tell, an answer which in fact we must make with regard to the Jewish Sabbath. But on what is my mind the more probable hypothesis, that the planetary week came into use a century or two before our era, we can see how a starting-point could be obtained. The astrologers who first conceived the idea of assigning hours in sequence to the planets had the Jewish precedent before them. On the theory that the Sabbath was really Saturn's day, it would be clear that the first hour of that day belonged to Saturn and the rest followed as a matter of course. There is also another possibility which I think should be mentioned, though I do not wish to lay much stress upon it. I have already said that Vettius Valens gives directions for finding the day of the week of any given day in any given year. I may now add that he takes as his basis the 'first year of Augustus,' and assumes that this began with a Sunday. Now we know from other sources that the reformed Egyptian calendar was dated from what is called the first year of Augustus, that is the year in which he entered Alexandria after his victory over Antony and Cleopatra. This entry actually took place on August 1st, 30 B.C., but as the Egyptian year begins with the month of Thoth, which almost coincides with our September, the Augustan era of Egypt was calculated from the 1st of Thoth 30 B.C. There has been some controversy as to whether this was August 30th or 31st. Mommsen (rightly, I believe) decided in favour of the latter, though he does not seem to have known the passage in Valens, which, I think, must decide the controversy finally. For any one who takes the trouble, and it is no more, to calculate[1],

---

[1] Those who have no access to chronological tables like those of Sir H. Nicholas or Mr J. J. Bond, and are unfamiliar with such calculations, may find the matter simplified by

will find that August 31st in that year actually
was what we call Sunday. Supposing then that
the idea of the planetary week was first conceived in Egypt (and we have to remember that
Dion says that it was) at a date later than 30 B.C.,
it would be natural that those who began the
observance should take as their starting-point
the first hour of their own era. They would still
have to decide which planet should start it, and
two answers might be given to this question. In
one sense the natural starting-point of the week
is either Saturn or the Moon, the two extremes
of the series, and we have seen that in Dositheus'
case and others it appears to be arranged from
Saturn downwards. In another sense, however,
the natural planet to lead is the Sun who, though
his throne is situated in the middle of the Seven,
is obviously king of them all. It is possible
therefore that Egyptian astrologers may have
assumed that their era began with the Sun and
the rest would follow automatically. My objection to this solution, which I find in many
ways tempting, is that it throws the origin of the
week very late. It would be certainly impossible
to square it with the ordinary interpretation of
the passage in Tibullus, for it is inconceivable

remembering that January 1st, A.D. 1 fell on Saturday, and also
that in the Julian calendar the days of the week recur on the
same days of the year after 28 years. Thus January 1st in
28 B.C. was Saturday, and as 29 B.C. was a leap-year January
1st in 30 B.C. was Wednesday. A few minutes' calculation,
if a calendar is not at hand, will of course give the rest.

that a usage which began after 30 B.C. should in
a very few years have obtained such a hold, that
an Italian poet should not only know it, but
utilize it in a poem which he intended to be
understood by the general reader. But I have
tried to shew that this ordinary interpretation is
not the only possible one, and since if we rule it
out we get no *certain* evidence of the week till
a time approaching A.D. 79, I think this possibility of dating the week from Sunday, August
31st, 30 B.C. is just worth consideration[1]. It
should, however, be remembered that, if it were
accepted, we should still have to regard the
coincidence of the Sabbath with the Saturn's
day of the new 'chronocratory' as a confirmatory
factor. If, on the other hand, we adopt my first
suggestion that the precedent of the Sabbath was
the *one* fact which gave the astrologers their
starting-point, we could throw the date considerably earlier. In fact, so far as this goes, the
planetary week might have originated at any

[1] It is an argument of some weight against this and indeed
against Dion's theory of the Egyptian origin of the planetary
week that the Alexandrian Jew Philo (*c.* 25 B.C.–A.D. 50) never
mentions the planetary days or hours. This is not an ordinary
case of negative evidence, for Philo several times and particularly in a special treatise on the number seven (*de septenario*)
ransacks the universe for examples of the predominance of the
sacred number. He certainly means to be exhaustive. But
while of course he dwells both on the number of the planets
and of the days of the week, he never brings the two into connexion. The fact is odd anyhow, but it would be odder still if
the system was pre-eminently Egyptian.

time not earlier than the firm establishment of the Jewish Dispersion as a substantial factor in history, a point which in Egypt at any rate is as early as the fourth century B.C.

And here I may appropriately add what little I have to say about the *further* antiquity of the institution, a question, be it observed, distinct from that of the antiquity of the week in general, that is of a seven or eight-day cycle not governed by planetary associations. We find no trace of the planetary week earlier than Tibullus, but absence of evidence is not evidence of absence, and I will not say that it is absolutely impossible that the sequence may have come down continuously from a remote age. But I believe that the supposition is improbable as well as unnecessary. In the first place there is nothing improbable in the view that the idea of a planetary chronocratory took shape not long before the time when we can first trace it. When we find a usage first coming to our knowledge in a certain period of history, we are justified in believing that it is a heritage from some remote past on two conditions. One is that we find a tradition that it comes from such earlier time. There is no trace of any such tradition in the case of the planetary week. On the contrary, the one statement which we have concerning its age, that of Dion Cassius, declares that it is recent. The other condition is that the usage shews signs of being a survival of ideas which have become obsolete. This condition is also wanting here. The planetary week clearly presupposes belief in astrology and in the planets in particular. But belief in the planets was not obsolete in the Roman Empire. On the contrary it was exceedingly vigorous, and there is not the slightest difficulty in supposing that the wave of astrological superstition which spread over the Mediterranean world, at a date which may be placed about 200 B.C., should have evolved the further idea that the planets presided in sequence over definite portions of time[1].

One misapprehension should be guarded against in this connexion. It is idle to deduce anything from the fact that reverence for or even worship of the planets is as old as the Babylonian records. That two of these, 'the greater light which rules the day, and the lesser light which rules the night,' should be the objects of awe and reverence to primitive man was inevitable, and when early observation discovered the fact that these moving bodies were not two but seven, the coincidence of this with the number of the stars in the Pleiades, the Great and Little Bear and

[1] I should add that the evidence which Rawlinson adduced from the walls of Ecbatana, as described by Herodotus i, 98, and the existing ruins of the temple at Borsippa, is now generally discarded. The idea was that the order of the colours was that of the planets in week-order. The order at Ecbatana is definitely not week-order, and that at Borsippa is quite uncertain. *V.* Jensen in *Zeitschrift für Deutsche Wortforschung*, 1901, pp. 157, 158.

other constellations may have done much, perhaps everything, to invest the number seven with special sanctity. But it does not in the least follow that because men recognize this they should proceed to map out time in perpetual sequences of planetary hours or days. Different nations have had their pantheons of it may be five or ten or any number of deities: they have not created weeks to represent them. Europe has for many centuries adored three Persons in the Godhead: it has not produced successive trinities of days. It has reverenced twelve apostles, but though the fact that there are twelve months in our calendar might easily have suggested the idea that each apostle should preside over each month in turn, this also has not been done. On the contrary, it seems to me that the instinct of men is towards intensiveness in these matters and that they feel they can best shew their reverence by concentrating it on special days which do not recur too frequently.

Hitherto we have been dealing with negative evidence, but there is one piece of positive evidence which goes far to shew that the observance of a planetary cycle is not a thing of immemorial antiquity. The hour sequence on which the day sequence of the week is founded, is, as we have seen, that of what we have called the normal order of the planets, running down from Saturn to the Moon with the Sun in the centre. The planetary week therefore both of day and hour can hardly be earlier than the date at which we find this order accepted. When was this? We have no clear evidence of it earlier than 200 or so B.C., but tradition in the first century A.D. ascribed the determination of this order to Pythagoras[1]. Even if this is correct, we still have no really ancient date, for Pythagoras belongs to the sixth century B.C. But we have to set against this tradition the fact that Plato who had strong sympathy with Pythagoras' teaching does not observe this order, as he places the Sun in the sixth and not the fourth place of the Seven. It is more important to observe that a different order is stated to be found in Babylonian and Egyptian records[2]. Here then we have something more than negative evidence: for it is difficult to believe that in Egypt and Chaldaea there were two theories current of the planetary order; one powerful enough to create a time-cycle, but leaving no impression that has survived in the monuments, the other recorded in the monuments, but evidently having no relation to the week. This is a very strong argument, and to my mind so far conclusive, that the theory of the later origin of the week must hold the field, unless or until some evidence to rebut

[1] Pliny, *Naturalis Historia*, II, 84.
[2] *V.* Boll on *Hebdomad* in Pauly-Wissowa, p. 2567; Cumont, *Astrology and Religion*, p. 163. I must remind the reader that this is a point on which I must accept the best authority I can get.

it is discovered in the monuments of the far
past.

If this view is accepted, the much discussed
question whether the original home of the institution was Egypt or Chaldaea becomes almost
meaningless. The week belongs to the international astrology of the world whose centre was
Rome. It is Chaldaean in so far, but only so far,
as all astrology was or was held to be Chaldaean.
If indeed we could place its origin so late as the
Augustan era of Egypt, we might call it
Egyptian. But this view, though I have stated
it for consideration, seems to me improbable.
No one in fact knew in Dion Cassius' time, any
more than anyone knows now, *where* the week
began. It is the fruit of a movement not of
a country. We may safely say that, so far as
the Empire is concerned, it spread from east
to west, not from west to east, but nothing
more.

Before I leave this subject of the antiquity of
the planetary week, I would repeat a little more
fully of the planetary type what I said of the week
in general—that the question of antiquity has
little to do with the problem before us. That
problem is how and why did the week diffuse
itself through the Roman Empire in countries
which had certainly for the most part known
nothing of it. As I have said, the nature of the
evidence which reveals its existence to us strongly
suggests that it was a movement of the masses,

and the masses when they embrace a novelty
do not ask whether it is ancient, or at any rate
genuinely ancient. If by any chance they want
antiquity, it can easily be invented. In fact, the
week time-cycle for our purpose was *new*, a new
development if not a new creation.

I have necessarily had to make this considerable digression from the primary subject of
this section, the relation of the Jewish to the
other type of week, and to this I now return.
The fact that the planetary type is properly one
of hours rather than days and that it is part of
a general system of time sovereignties makes
it impossible to my mind to look on it as a mere
variation of the Jewish or Sabbatical type. The
ideas at the bottom of the two are radically different. Yet I have no doubt that they are closely
intertwined. Apart from my suggestion that the
Sabbath afforded a starting-point for the planetary series, it was natural that astrologers imbued
with the idea that the Sabbath was Saturn's day
should think of the Jewish week as a variation
of their own. We have an incidental sign of this
in Valens himself. He has two names for 'week
day.' One is 'Hebdomad,' a word which can
mean either 'seven' or the 'seventh' in a series;
the other is Sabbatic-day. As I have already
suggested Sabbatarianism and Planetism must
have supported and reacted on each other, and
not only must we suppose that proselytes to
Judaism entered with planetary associations of

which they did not easily rid themselves, but it is possible that planetary conceptions of the week, which are certainly to be found in later Rabbinic literature, had already begun to influence the Jews themselves. Whether we can find any trace of the kind in the early Christian Church will be the subject of the sixth section.

§ 5

THE DRIVING-FORCE BEHIND
THE WEEK

We now come to a different question. How did the planetary week gain its ascendancy in the Empire? I do not think that the difficulty of this has been properly appreciated. We talk glibly of one nation 'getting it' from another, but as a matter of fact a new time-cycle is not a thing which spreads automatically. The most natural method of propagation is by official authority. Let those in power conceive the idea that the innovation is useful and take steps to bring it into force, and no doubt the rest is easy. That is the way in which great reforms in the calendar, such as the Julian or Gregorian, have been established, or in recent years our own 'summer time.' But as we have seen there is complete silence as to any official enforcement or even recognition of the planetary week, and this is a matter in which silence does imply non-existence. Shall we then say it was just a fashion? Fashion is in many ways no doubt extremely creative. It can produce revolutions in costume, new varieties of speech and indeed new religious observances. But a new time-cycle is a much more difficult matter.

How do we ourselves remember the days of

the week? The obvious answer is that something happens on one or more of them. If by some means or other we lose count in the course of the week, Sunday is unmistakable, even if personally we have no religious feeling about the day. So, too, school half-holiday or early-closing days force themselves on the notice of those who are not directly affected by them. But if nothing happens it is very doubtful whether a week-sequence could maintain, much less establish, itself. I have not had any opportunity of finding out what is the experience of parties or individuals, such as explorers or hunters, if they are cut off from civilization for any length of time. But I observe that writers of fiction which deals with this type of adventure have felt that week-keeping would be a difficulty. Both Robinson Crusoe and that pious Protestant pastor the hero of the *Swiss Family Robinson* were strict Sabbatarians. But even they missed a Sunday or two, though I think they took steps later to prevent a recurrence of this.

But in the planetary week nothing, so far as we know, happened. Nothing in the heaven above: the planets rolled on their courses regardless of the days assigned to them. Nothing on the earth below: there was, as we have seen, no official or civil recognition, and outside Jew, Christian and possibly Mithraist, we know of no formal rite or meeting. We can only suppose that the plain man who did not belong to these

bodies rose in the morning and passed the day
with a definite consciousness that it was in some
way or other under the influence of a particular
one of the mysterious Seven.

One limitation must of course be made to
this. When a usage like the planetary week has
reached a certain point of acceptance, it is carried
further by its own momentum. When a majority of the community, or perhaps even a large
and solid minority has adopted it from conviction, the rest may accept it otiosely from mere
convenience. If the customer thinks in week-
days, the shopman who ministers to his needs
must at least learn to understand him. Some
considerable time before the general acceptance,
to which Dion testifies, had become a fact, the
week-days had probably come to be taken for
granted without much serious thought by a
large body of people. But in the earlier stages
when conviction not convenience was the only
motive we must, I think, postulate some very
strong driving-force, *Glaube* or *Aberglaube*, to
maintain among widely isolated groups or persons this new form of time-measurement, which
if once lost by a single lapse would be lost for
ever[1].

The general nature of this driving-force has

[1] One would suppose that in Italy or Rome at any rate it
must have required some strong influence to establish the planetary week of seven days against the Roman week of eight days.
It must surely be difficult to keep two weeks going at the same

been partially explained by what has been said about the time sovereignty of the planets, and it may be better understood, or perhaps I should say that the difficulty of understanding it will be better appreciated, when we have considered the history of the astrological movement during this period.

Divination by means of the heavenly bodies was not a primitive idea with either the Greeks or the Romans. Their superstitions took rather the form of auguries from the flight of birds, or from the entrails of slaughtered animals, and of dream-interpretation and various omens. There is no astrology in Homer or the Greek dramatists. It was perhaps the contact of East and West brought about by Alexander's armies which set the ball rolling. The universal belief in the Roman world that astrology was 'Chaldaean' in origin is probably so far true that the cruder astrological ideas of Babylon were grafted on to Greek astronomy to produce the elaborate system which prevailed to the Middle Ages. But there is, so far as I know, no historical evidence of its prevalence in the Empire of Alexander and his successors till the time when the Greek in his

time! I do not indeed know how much evidence there is of the observance of the nundinae after the first century or so. But market-days are always a persistent matter; moreover in the earlier times they regulated school holidays (*v.* Marquardt, *loc. cit.* p. 3). Superstition too attached to them. Augustus would take no journey on the day after the 'nundinae' (Suetonius, *Aug.* 92).

c

turn succumbed to the domination of Rome.
The earliest historical mention is, I believe, the
warning of Cato in his book on agriculture (in
the first half of the second century B.C.) to the
farmer against consulting the 'Chaldaean,' and
in 139 B.C. an edict was passed expelling them
from Italy. These facts of course presuppose
some prolonged period, during which the movement had time to acquire sufficient force to
become dangerous; and before Cato, the most
influential of the philosophical sects, the Stoics,
who certainly had afterwards a considerable
leaning to astrology, may have shewn this tendency. In the first century B.C. the mentions
become more frequent. Sulla, for instance, had
an astrological prediction forecasting his death.
Cicero deals with astrology in his book on divination. His contemporary Posidonius, an important name in the history of Stoicism, did
much to give a philosophical form to the belief.
When we come to the end of that century and
the beginning of our era, we have Augustus
publishing his 'theme of geniture' and using it
in his coinage[1], while Virgil bases on it an elaborate bit of flattery in the opening of his *Georgics*.
Manilius writes a didactic poem on astrology.
Horace alludes to the competing influences of
Jupiter and Saturn[2] and assures Maecenas that
their two stars are indissolubly bound together.

[1] Suetonius, *Aug.* 94.
[2] *Odes*, ii, 17, 17–24. Cf. 'Babylonios,' numeros i, 11, 2.

Propertius' allusions are still fuller. Later again
we hear of astrological predictions in connexion
with Tiberius, Nero, Vespasian, Titus and
Domitian, while Juvenal launches his satire
against the ladies who regulate every action by
their astrological books[1]. Above all we read
frequently of edicts against astrologers and astrology, a superstition which Tacitus says will
always be forbidden and always retained in the
Roman state. All this evidence, which is merely
a selection from what is available, undoubtedly
shews that astrology had made very great head-
way during these centuries, but it does not to my
mind completely account for such a phenomenon
as the establishment of the week.

In the first place, striking as is the rapid
spread of astrological belief during this period,
when we compare it with the complete absence
of any such ideas in earlier times, it must not be
exaggerated. The evidence we get is largely of
the nature of gossip about great persons. It is
no doubt more than could be accumulated by
future historians with regard to any single one
of what I may, I hope with the minimum offence,
call the eccentricities of our time. But if
we combined these 'eccentricities'—Christian
science, theosophy, spiritualism, the various
forms of fortune-telling, and psycho-analysis—
a considerable body of proof of their currency
could be collected from memoirs, newspapers

[1] *Sat.* vi, 553 ff.

and the like. Yet no one would suppose that these really touched the general life of the people or were capable of bringing into existence a new time-cycle. So with the astrological movement there is no evidence apart from the week that it went down to the bed-rock of life. A simple test of this may be obtained by comparing the quantity of the allusions to astrology in Augustan literature with that of the allusions to the accepted theology or mythology. In the *Odes* of Horace the names of the gods appear on about every page: to astrology there are, I think, just two allusions. Much the same may be said of Virgil and in various degrees of every other poet, except of course Manilius. The one fact which, outweighing all the rest, testifies to the popular belief in planetary influence is the silent diffusion of the week.

Secondly, though obviously the week is connected with astrology, the tie that connects them is exceedingly loose. Though the idea of time sovereignty is an outcome of the belief that the planets control human destinies and could only be propagated where that belief had taken root, it is only a popular or semi-popular extension. Consequently in the lore of astrology proper it plays no great part. In the catalogues of the astrologers, which I mentioned in the last section, and in Vettius Valens, there is enough to shew us what the astrologers made of the week—enough to shew us that they regarded it as a system of hours as well as, or more than, of days: but these notices are only occasional. Still more significant is the fact that the full-dress refutations of astrology contain, so far as I know, not a single mention of the week system, though obviously, if it was regarded as a serious factor in astrology, it was a peculiarly vulnerable factor. Since the relations of Saturn to the other planets vary from Saturday to Saturday, how can Saturn have the same effect on human life, whenever this day recurs? The question was unanswerable; yet it is never asked. We have two such full-dress refutations which follow what were no doubt familiar lines of argument. One is a remarkable and interesting discussion by Sextus Empiricus, a writer of the later half of the second century A.D., who set himself to shew that all branches of learning were equally unreliable[1]. The other is in St Augustine's great treatise on *The City of God*[2]. Both deal with the contradictions to common sense involved in astrology, such as how, if it were true, could twins born under the same aspect of heaven have different destinies, as they do have. The fact that they do not mention the still greater absurdities involved in week observance shews that in their eyes it was hardly a part of astrological science, rather a vague popular superstition which did not need refutation.

The sort of place that the week held in the estimation of later astrologers, at any rate, may

---

[1] *Contra mathematicos*, v.   [2] *De Civitate Dei*, v.

perhaps be fairly judged from a curious incident in a later century[1]. In the reign of Zeno A.D. 484 a rebel general named Leontius had himself crowned and proclaimed Emperor at sunrise on the 27th of June. He had chosen the time on skilled astrological advice. The sun was in Cancer 26°, Venus in Gemini 27°, and so on for the other planets with other astronomical data. The general conjunction was eminently favourable. All the same the attempt was a complete fiasco, and the astrologers were much disconcerted. Further consideration, however, led to the reflection that no account had been taken of the fact that the hour chosen was the first hour of Wednesday, when Mercury is regent of both hour and day; Mercury's position was apparently unfavourable in itself and might therefore be regarded as outweighing the other favourable elements. Thus the science was vindicated though at the expense of the unhappy Leontius. In this story the week appears as a sort of inferior ally, whose assistance in ordinary cases may be dispensed with, but may be called in in emergencies to save the situation.

---

[1] I take this story from Bouché-Leclercq, *L'Astrologie Grecque*, pp. 514, 515. He gets it from a manual written by an astrologer named Palchus, which I have not seen. This manual, which apparently is more or less contemporary with the incident described, has been edited by Cumont (*v*. Bouché-Leclercq, p. xiv). I should add that Palchus found another flaw in the calculation of the astrologers, which does not concern our subject.

In this case it will be observed that we have a sort of combination of astrology proper with week-lore. No universal rules are laid down for Wednesdays, but the observer is bidden to remember that Mercury is paramount in the first hour of Wednesday and then to note the positions of Mercury on that particular Wednesday and to shape his course accordingly, and this is the line taken by our earliest authority Valens. This is perhaps a trifle more rational than what we find in other authorities, who seem to hold that the laws for each hour of each day in the week are irrevocably fixed and have no reference to what may be the particular position of the paramount planets on any particular hour or day. One specimen of this stuff will, I think, be enough[1]. I will take the hour at which I am writing, namely, about 12.30 midday of Friday, November 20th, 1925. As the sun rises about 7.30 a.m. and sets shortly after 4 p.m., the day-hours are about 43 minutes each, and we are now in the eighth of them according to the western astrological reckoning. Venus is therefore regent of both the day and the hour. The authority before me gives me advice as to four contingencies and four only. My slave may run away (this is a possibility the astrologers seem regularly to provide for): I may fall ill: I may lose or break something, or I may have a thief. During this particular hour, I find that if the

[1] *Cat. Cod. Astr. Graec.* vii, pp. 88 ff.

slave absconds, he will either hide in my sub-
urban farm, or in a public house with a woman:
if I fall ill, I shall have a hard time, but shall
recover: if I lose anything, it will be elegant ear-
rings, and my thief will be a 'softish womanish
kind of person.'[1] In a half-hour or so of our
time, we shall enter the next astrological hour,
which is Mercury's, though Venus is still regent
of the day. My runaway in that case will take
refuge in 'the church of the martyrs': if I fall ill,
I shall die: my lost property will be parchments
or gilded vessels, and the thief will be an
educated or literary person.

It will be seen that in all this week-lore,
whether of the fantastic kind just described, the
comparative lateness of which is shewn by such
phrases as 'the church of the martyrs,' or in the
more sober form which Valens gives it, the hour
counts for as much as, if not more, than the day,
and it is clear that this was the view taken in
esoteric astrological circles down to the days of
Chaucer. But I very much doubt whether the
hour business had any hold on the popular mind.
To them the week was a system of seven
planetary days, not of 168 planetary hours. I
judge this from the fact that the planet-hours
have left no impression on language and also
from the way in which Dion speaks of them. He
knows that the hours are said to be dedicated to
the planets, but he only knows it as a theory.

[1] γυναικώδης μαλακώδης.

The ascription of each day to a planet is to him a matter of universal knowledge. If the ascription of each hour to a planet had been an equally accepted fact, he would not have needed to give his explanation at all.

If the people had no hour-lore had they any definite day-lore? Did they think that illnesses ran a different course according to the days on which they were contracted, or that Friday's thief would be of a different stamp to Wednesday's? I know of only one scrap of evidence which bears on this, and it is a very little scrap and does not come from the earliest period. Ausonius[1], a poet and scholar of the fourth century, a Christian by profession, though with much or more of the pagan about him, quotes a proverbial line

> Cut nails on Mercury's day,
> Beard on Jupiter's day,
> Hair on Venus's day,

and proceeds in a little set of verses to refute this on the grounds that Mercury being the god of thieves presumably approves of sharp nails, that Jupiter is represented with a beard and Venus with long hair, and that therefore these are the wrong days for these several processes. The verses are not seriously meant and are only relevant in so far as they are founded on what we may by a stretch call a piece of folk-lore bearing

[1] *Ecloga*, 26.

on the week. On the whole we must say that we do not know what in practice the week meant to the plain man of the Empire. Yet we know that he learnt to observe it and must conclude that he had some motive for doing so, whether it took any practical form or not.

Another question which may be asked is whether the spread of the week is due in whole or in part to its being included in the ritual of particular sects or religions. I have already said that the planetary week no doubt received much support from the Sabbatical week of the Jews. So, too, the Christian acceptance of the seven-day week may have helped: though its contribution in the second century must have been small. But there is another religion which may have contributed, if not to establish, at any rate to widen its influence. That religion is Mithraism. We have heard of late years much of the various mystery religions, of the rites of Isis, Cybele, Attis and Adonis, but perhaps none has attracted so much attention as that of the Persian Sun-god Mithras. Many striking suggestions have been made about it. We are told that there was a time when it was an even chance whether Christianity or Mithraism would become the dominant religion of the Empire, and that the fixing of the feast of the Nativity of Christ close to the winter solstice was made in imitation of the Mithraistic feast in celebration of the annual birth of the Sun-god. Mr H. G. Wells in his

Outline of History has assured us positively that the Christians 'borrowed Sunday from the Mithraists.'[1] Whether sober enquiry will establish all or many of these statements remains, I think, to be seen. But at any rate the wide diffusion of Mithraism in Europe, particularly in the army, is an interesting fact.

That Mithraism should adopt week-observance when it had become general elsewhere was clearly inevitable. A religion in which the supreme object of adoration was so closely connected if not identified with the Sun could hardly fail to pay special reverence to what even non-Mithraists hailed as the Sun's day, even if it did not pay the same regard to the other planets; and when the recurrence of one day in seven is observed, we have of course the week. Cumont's statement[2] therefore that the week and especially Sunday was observed by the Mithraists, is thoroughly credible, whatever we may think of the evidence which he gives. The real question for us is to what date we can trace the Mithraistic week. Mithraism, according to

[1] I presume that Mr Wells found this statement in some respectable authority. But he did not get it from Cumont, who, after remarking that the Mithraists like the Christians specially observed Sunday (though he gives no evidence for it), goes on: 'Mithraism cannot have had any influence on Christianity in this, for the substitution of Sunday for the Sabbath dates from apostolic times.'

[2] *Textes et monuments figurés relatifs aux mystères de Mithra*, I, pp. 119, 325, 339.

Cumont, grew to some influence in the Roman Empire during the first century A.D. and reached the height of its strength in the third. Are we to regard it as taking the lead in the spread of week-observance, or merely as being carried along in the general current and adapting its rites to its environment? We find, I think, no evidence which would lead us to take the former view. The positive indications adduced by Cumont seem on examination to be exceedingly slight. A Mithraeum at Ostia[1] is said to have the figures of the Seven and below them semi-circular stations from which Cumont supposes that the priest invoked the planet of the day. But the figures are *not* in week-order. A bas-relief undoubtedly Mithraean found in Bologna[2] does give them in week-sequence, but, if read in the ordinary way from left to right, they run Sun, Saturn, Venus, Jupiter, Mercury, Mars, Moon. This sculpture, therefore, to which Cumont does not assign a date, has the week-gods, but in an inverted order. Much the same appears in the one literary passage on which Cumont relies to prove week-knowledge in Mithraism. This is in Origen's famous refutation of the attack made on Christianity by an otherwise unknown person called Celsus[3]. It is

---

[1] *Textes et monuments figurés relatifs aux mystères de Mithra,* I, p. 114.   [2] *Ib.*
[3] Origen, *Contra Celsum,* VI, 21. This passage is printed in full in *Textes et monuments,* II, p. 31.

hardly necessary to say that we only know
Celsus' treatise by what Origen says of it, and
we cannot always be sure that he represents it
fairly. But the passage in question seems to be a
definite quotation and may be taken to represent
justly at any rate what Celsus, a non-Mithraist,
had been told about Mithraistic belief. According to this the pilgrimage of the human soul
from a lower to a higher state was symbolized
by a ladder composed of seven portals with an
eighth at the top. These seven portals were represented by different metals each corresponding
to a planet, and the order in which these came
was Saturn, Venus, Jupiter, Mercury, Mars,
Moon, Sun. Celsus, says Origen, 'to shew off
his learning' added 'unnecessary' explanations
of the order of the planets, and as one of the
explanations is described as connected with the
theory of music, we may fairly assume that it is
the same as the first of Dion's two explanations.
Here then, as in Bologna, we have the week-
order reversed, but with the difference that,
whereas that began with the Sun and ended with
the Moon, here we begin with Saturn and end
with the Sun. In the one case the week begins
with Sunday and ends with Monday, in the other
it begins with Saturday and ends with Sunday.
Apart from this somewhat serious departure
from the normal week, we have to remember
that the date is late for our present purpose. It
is true that though Origen is supposed to have

written his treatise about A.D. 250, the book he
is answering was not of recent origin, but it is
not usually dated earlier than A.D. 180. We
have thus no certainty that even if the slight and
vague evidences just mentioned are to be connected with the week, they represent a time
anterior to that at which we know it to have been
in general use, when Mithraism, as I have said,
with its prepossessions could hardly fail to adopt
it. All we can say, then, is that as the week
spread, it would find sympathy and support from
Mithraism, which in this way may well have
done something to swell the volume of popular
feeling which propagated the new time-cycle.

As to the other 'mystery religions,' we may
presume that they followed the popular current
in conforming to week-observance. There is
nothing in what we know of their creeds or the
mentality of their devotees that would run
counter to it. But I am not aware that there is
anything *positive* to connect them with it. And
the same, I think, though I would speak with
all caution, may be said of that vast and vague
body of belief and practice which we call magic.
Magic and astrology went no doubt to a great
extent hand in hand. For though originally and
in logic they were opponents, since magic aims
at a control of the destiny, which astrology
declares to be beyond our control, in practice it
was not so. The mind, which comes under the
sense of this overwhelming power, will always

be clutching at some method of propitiating or
eluding it. It is not surprising, therefore, that
we should find among the remains of magical
documents occasional incantations to the planets,
and that these should sometimes shew recognition of the planetary hours or days. These may
very likely be much more numerous than those
which I can give from my present knowledge.
One of the volumes of those 'Codices Astro-
logorum' which I have already quoted contains
a number of magic formulae of an astrological
type[1]. These direct the spell to be used when
one or other of the planets is in a certain position
in the Zodiac. But there is also appended a
direction that it shall be used at the 'hour' of
some planet, which is frequently a different one
from that whose position is described. In these
formulae the 'hour' of the planet may be assumed to mean the hour or hours in the planetary week which belong to the planet in question.
No mention is made of days, and we have here
an indication that, while to the popular mind the
planet-days were the essential thing, the esoteric mind thought more of the hours which
were the original unit of the system. Again, an
Egyptian magical papyrus now in the Leyden
Museum has side by side the normal and the
week-order of the planets[2]. The former is headed
the 'Seven-Zones,' the other simply 'Greek,' a
fact which, by the way, does not encourage us

[1] iii, pp. 40 ff.   [2] *V*. Schürer, p. 24.

to think that in Egypt itself the week was regarded as Egyptian in origin. Some 'cursing'
tablets also have been found in Rome, in which
'Mars' day' is recognized as unlucky[1]. But in
none of these cases does there appear to be any
adequate[2] reason for thinking that they belong
to a date previous to the complete establishment
of the week, and therefore all they shew, as in
the case of Mithraism, is that when the planetary
days or hours lay ready to hand, magic made
use of them. Possibly better evidence may
be or may already have been discovered and
therefore, as I said, I speak with caution. But
until such evidence is produced, the above is the
best opinion we can form.

To the fact, then, that the planetary week
established itself without official recognition, we
have to add the probability that it established
itself with little reference to any astrological
body of doctrine, or to any existing religion,
except indirectly to Judaism. The plain man who
learnt to reckon time in these planetary terms
did not, so far as we can tell, acknowledge any
definite law of what to do or what not to do on
each day of the week. And we have again to ask
the question, what was the driving-force which

[1] *V*. Schürer, p. 24.
[2] Dieterich, who reproduces the Leyden papyrus in his
Abraxas, thought that the contents pointed to a second century
origin. But he admitted that the papyrus itself belonged to the
third or fourth.

led vast multitudes to adopt silently this time-
cycle, which—let me once more reiterate this
point—was new to them, whether it actually
originated in recent or in prehistoric times. We
cannot, I think, do more than say that it grew
because the plain man believed vaguely but pro-
foundly in the power of the planets. He rose on
Friday and Saturday with the belief that these
days were somehow under the influence, the one
of the beneficent, the other of the maleficent
star. He did not know what either could do for
him, or what the astrologers said about them,
but as other people remembered them, it was
well for him to remember them also. And he
was confirmed in this view by the belief that
that remarkable, if objectionable, people, the
Jews, appeared to attach immense importance to
abstinence from activity on Saturn's day. This
is the only answer I can give. I am not sure that
it is a satisfactory one: at any rate it leaves me
with a sense of some mystery surrounding the
whole institution. One thing, however, is clear.
The institution of the week remains to shew us,
as nothing else in the history of the astrological
movement does, how widely diffused and deeply
rooted in the early Empire was the belief in the
all-mastering power of the planets.

6

THE WEEK IN THE NEW TESTAMENT
AND THE EARLY CHURCH

The New Testament shews little sign of the great astrological movement of those times. It is true that at the very outset of the Gospels we find a story in which Chaldaean astrologers have learnt by a star that a King of the Jews has been born, but the details added, namely that the star accompanies them and finally indicates the house in which the Child lay, have no relation to the regular creed of astrology. In fact the story, though, as far as it goes, it regards astrological divination with a favour which caused considerable searchings of heart among some of the Fathers, does not suggest that the writer knew anything more than that Chaldaean sages were credited with a power of interpreting the stars. In the Acts the absence of allusions to astrology is very marked. We are apt to forget that this book, or at least the latter part of it, is an authority of the first importance not only for the history of the primitive Church but for some aspects of general social life in the provinces of the Empire. There is in fact no parallel to it in what we call the secular literature of the time—nothing, that is, which gives us a similar picture by a man of the people of the life of the people.

In the Acts we hear a good deal about magic: we have two sorcerers, Simon and Elymas. But the most remarkable example is the curious story in the 19th chapter. Here we first find some Jews acting as 'exorcists,' practising, that is, a comparatively innocent and beneficent form of magic against evil demons, and attempting to use the name of Jesus with disastrous results to themselves. And this so impresses the inhabitants of Ephesus, that they determine in large numbers to give up magical practices, and bring their magical books to be burnt, the writer adding the curious fact that their value was definitely estimated at over £1700 of our money. An interesting touch is added by the statement that many of the converts to Christianity were fain to confess that they had been dabbling in magic, shewing, what indeed we might expect, that the ordinary convert did not at once throw off his original superstitions. In all this there is no word of astrology. It is possible indeed that as 'mage' was a term used indifferently for sorcerer and astrologer, we may be intended to understand that Simon and Elymas combined both arts, and the Ephesian books may have included astrological spells, like those mentioned at the end of the last section. But this is a very different thing from formal or scientific astrology, and the complete absence of this in the Acts goes

a good way to confirm me in the view that astrology in the proper sense had not gone down
to the bed-rock of life. Nor, except possibly in
two passages which will require separate discussion, does Paul shew either favour or hos-
tility to astrology, though he, too, denounces
magic in the Epistle to the Galatians as one of
the works of the flesh, just as the author of the
Revelation classes the sorcerer with fornicators
and idolaters. Paul's talk about 'principalities
and powers,' 'world-rulers of darkness,' the
'prince of the power of the air' and the like does
indeed seem to shew that he conceived of the sky
as peopled by a host of demons, and he may
possibly have conceived of them as identical
with or located in the stars and planets[1], but
there is nothing to shew that this is so. An
attempt indeed has been made in the great passage of Romans viii, where he enumerates the
powers which can never 'separate him from the
love of God which is in Christ Jesus our Lord,'
to take the words 'height' and 'depth' to mean

[1] This is in itself a natural idea. As Christians who looked
with favour on astrology might identify the planets with angels
(*v. infra*, p. 98) so those who held the system in abomination
might identify them with demons. Have we not possibly a
hint of this in the one passage in the N.T. where the planets
are mentioned (Jude 13)? There the deceivers of the Church
are called 'wandering stars (ἀστέρες πλανῆται) to whom
the blackness of darkness is reserved for ever.' The diabolical
powers who now shine so brightly will be plunged with their
devotees into eternal night.

respectively the 'ascension' and 'declination' of
the stars[1]. The Greek words can be used in this
astronomical sense, but the ordinary interpretation is philologically just as likely, and most of
us will feel it incongruous to introduce this
rather bizarre idea into what is perhaps the
grandest flight of eloquence in the whole of the
Pauline writings.

The only book of the New Testament in
which it is at all possible to trace any familiarity
with astrology is the Revelation, and, while
many critics like Dr Charles wholly deny its
presence there, others, like the German professors
Lepsius[2] and Boll[3], contend that the book is
saturated in astrological ideas. The former, for
instance, suggested that the seven angels of the
seven churches in the first three chapters symbolize the seven planets, though not in week-
order, while the four horsemen of chapter vi
become the four planets Moon, Mars, Mercury
and Jupiter. Venus and Saturn follow somehow
and we finally come to the angel standing in the
Sun. Boll, on the other hand, appealing to the
fact that there was a chronocratory of the Zodiac
as well as of the planets and that thus there were
cycles of twelve years, in each of which a sign of
the Zodiac presided, identifies the four horse-

---

[1] Reitzenstein, *Poimandres*, p. 80.
[2] In some articles written in English with an introduction
by Professor Ramsay in the *Expositor*, 1911 (i).
[3] *Hellenistische Studien zu Weltbild der Apocalypse.*

men with the constellations of the Lion, Virgin, Scales and Scorpion. He certainly adduces some curious similarities between the properties which were supposed by the astrologers to belong to these four signs and those which are shewn by the horsemen. In the same way he interprets the mysterious woman of chapter xii, who, clothed with the sun and with the moon under her feet and crowned with the twelve stars, gives birth to a child, as the central sign of the Virgin, and suggests that one form of interpretation of Isaiah's words 'Behold the Virgin shall conceive, etc.' was that this great constellation, thought of, of course, as a divine or angelic being, would be the mother of the Messiah. Those who are interested in these speculations will certainly find Boll suggestive. I do not say that they will find him convincing.

Hitherto even the little evidence we have found has been mainly concerned with astrology itself and not with that popular and loosely connected product of astrology, the planetary week. The ordinary student of the New Testament, who is not likely to discover for himself the subtleties of Boll and Lepsius, would probably say that there is no trace to be found in it of any knowledge of the planetary cycle. Yet, apart from these possibilities and some others which I shall suggest from the Epistles to the Galatians and Colossians, there is one momentous fact in the history of the Church which deserves at any

rate serious consideration in this connexion. I
mean the change by which the Church adopted
as its day of meeting the first instead of the
seventh in the Jewish week—the Sun's day
instead of Saturn's day in the planetary system.

We have, of course, glimpses of this change
in the New Testament itself. In the Acts we are
told that the Christians of Troas met on the first
day of the week for the 'breaking of bread.'[1]
Paul himself bids the Corinthians lay aside their
contributions for the relief of the Church at
Jerusalem on that day[2], and though he does not
expressly mention a meeting, it is reasonable to
conclude that they were collected at a meeting.
The writer of the Apocalypse sees his vision on
'the Lord's day,'[3] and though many sober critics
have thought that this means the day on which
the Lord appeared to the seer, or the day of
Judgment which he saw in vision, it does not
seem to me reasonable to doubt that he means
Sunday, in face of the fact that this name for
Sunday is undoubtedly found some thirty years
later and remained afterwards in universal use.

The meagre Christian literature which bridges
over the gap between the writings of the New
Testament and Justin contains several allusions
to the festival or meeting-day on the first day of
the week. Ignatius in one of the famous letters[4]
which he addressed to various Churches as he

[1] xx, 7.   [2] 1 Cor. xvi, 2.
[3] i, 10.   [4] Ignatius, *ad Magnesios*, 9.

was brought to martyrdom from Antioch to
Rome speaks of his Jewish converts 'as no
longer observing Sabbaths, but living in
accordance with the Lord's day, on which also
our life rose through him and his death.' The
so-called *Epistle of Barnabas* ends a long and
fantastic disquisition about Sabbaths (to which I
shall recur) by saying 'that for this reason' (i.e.
that which he has just mentioned) 'we observe
the eighth day for joy, on which also Jesus rose
from the dead and, after manifesting Himself,
ascended to heaven.'[1] The *Teaching of the Twelve
Apostles* bids the Church meet on the 'Lord's
day of the Lord' to break bread or hold the
Eucharist[2]. I need not go into the date of these
documents further than to say that probably
everyone would reckon them as earlier than
Justin. His statement, which is by far the clearest, I have already quoted. We cannot in fact
doubt for a moment that the Church from a very
early date adopted the practice of meeting on
what to the Jews was the first day of the week,
to the general public the Sun's day, and to the
Christians themselves the Lord's day; and it is
hardly less clear that the predominant reason
they assigned for this at any rate in the second century was that it commemorated the Resurrection.

[1] Ch. 15. 'Barnabas' seems to follow the version of the
Ascension in Luke xxiv where it appears to be placed on Easter
Day rather than that of Acts i, where it occurs 40 days after.
So too does pseudo-Jerome quoted on p. 94.   [2] Ch. 14.

At the same time it is obvious that the reason which was assigned in the second century for the observance of Sunday may not have been the original reason, or at any rate the sole original reason. It is probable enough that the infant Church, entirely composed of Jews, may have been led by some motive of convenience, which we cannot now discover, to its choice of a day. It was natural at any rate that they should choose some other day than the Sabbath and leave that free for the worship of the Synagogue. When the Church spread it is quite conceivable that the practice might have been changed, but that the day had already acquired a certain sanctity, and one of the causes of this sanctity I cannot doubt was the feeling that it commemorated the Resurrection. But was there another cause, namely, that it was the Sun's day?[1]

The French 'modernist' Loisy has adopted

---

[1] The degree of importance to be attributed to this consideration will no doubt largely depend on the currency which we suppose the planetary week to have obtained during the period in which the Lord's day was becoming an unquestioned and sacred element in Christian life. Now we certainly must not assume, and indeed I think it is improbable, that at this period, which may roughly be regarded as covering the later decades of the first and the earlier decades of the second century, the week had obtained anything like the general recognition of Dion's time. On the other hand it probably had all the vigour of a growing institution, and also we may suppose that the temperament which led men at one part of their lives to planetary devotion, would often lead them at another to Christianity.

this view unhesitatingly[1]. He seems indeed to
go further and hold that the story that the Resurrection took place on the first day of the week
was an afterthought. He does not, I imagine,
doubt that the Church from the first believed
that her risen Master had appeared to his disciples, or that this belief was the foundation of
the Gospel. But he thinks that the story of the
tomb being found empty on the first day of the
week, and the placing of the first appearances
on the same day arose from an *a priori* conviction
that the Resurrection must have happened on
what had become the Lord's day, whereas in reality
it had become the Lord's day, because, as being
the 'principal day' of the week and the day of the
chief of the great Seven, it seemed to be especially
suited for the service of the Lord of Glory.

My readers will probably agree with me that
this extreme theory is as improbable as it is
arbitrary. The belief that Jesus rose on the day
after the Sabbath belongs to the earliest form of
the Gospel narrative. For though Mark breaks
off without relating any appearances, and quite
possibly in the lost conclusion did not record
any as happening till the disciples returned to
Galilee, he clearly states that the Resurrection
had taken place when the women arrived at the
tomb. Further an earlier witness than Mark,
namely Paul, practically says the same thing,

---

[1] *Les Mystères Païens,* pp. 223-229.

when he tells the Corinthians that the Lord 'rose again on the third day.' But without going so far or nearly so far as Loisy, we may reasonably think that the planetary associations of the day may, perhaps almost must, have contributed to its sanctity and do something to account for an institution, the origin of which is in fact somewhat obscure, or at any rate requires rather more consideration than it usually receives.

For in the first place we may ask whether a weekly commemoration of any event is a natural proceeding. The instinct of men in these matters is as I have said intensive. We prefer to keep yearly commemorations. Friday, it is true, is a fast-day, but otherwise the Church does not commemorate the Crucifixion every week. No one wishes for a weekly Christmas. In secular matters no one proposes to celebrate weekly the detection of the Gunpowder Plot or Armistice Day or his own birthday. As a matter of fact the day of the week on which these events occurred is known to no one (unless he takes the trouble to investigate it) in the case of the first, to few in the case of the second and almost as few in the case of the third. But a more important consideration is that, though the predominant reason assigned in the second century is the Resurrection, it is not the only one. Justin, in the passage quoted above, couples with the Resurrection the beginning of creation, and elsewhere, thinking of Sunday as the eighth day, he

connects it with the law by which the circumcision of the child took place on the eighth day
from birth[1]. Barnabas, though he speaks of it
as the day on which *also* Christ rose, and, he
adds, ascended, gives as the primary reason a
theory, which is found also in the '*Slavonic*'
Enoch[2], that there have been six millenniums
in the world's history, that in the seventh the
old world will be destroyed, while in the eighth,
the true Lord's day, the new life will begin.
Ignatius' language, too, is somewhat obscure.
When he speaks of the Lord's day as the day
on which 'also our life *rose* through him and
his death,' he uses a verb which is regularly
applied to the rising of the heavenly bodies and
not that which is commonly used of resurrection
from the dead[3]. And it is certainly not impossible
that he has at the back of his mind the conception
of Christ as the true Sun, the 'day-spring from
on high,' as much as of the Resurrection itself.

Now if we believe, as I think we must, that
Christianity and the observance of the planetary
week spread more or less contemporaneously
and over the same areas, and also that this new
time-cycle could not establish itself without some

[1] Dialogue with Trypho, ch. 41.
[2] Ch. 33. Also in Augustine, *De Civitate Dei*, xxii, 30, 5,
with some adaptations.
[3] ἀνέτειλεν not ἀνέστη. He too like Barnabas inserts the
'also' which may perhaps indicate some uncertainty as to the
origin of the practice.

strong belief in planetary influences, however
vague, it is impossible that Gentile converts
should have thrown off the associations which
had gathered round the Sun's day. We have
seen how the Acts testifies to the difficulty which
they found in abjuring magical practices. And
while magic was clearly anti-Christian, the same
could hardly be said of the planetary week. Some
indeed might hold, as in later days many undoubtedly did, that the employment of the
planetary names implied worship of the deities
to which they were assigned and was therefore
idolatrous, but others might put on it a more
innocent construction; and a very natural view
was that the coincidence of Lord's day and Sun's
day was a proof that in this pagan institution the
Divine Spirit had been preparing the world for
something better. In fact, the devout convert
might well rejoice to be able to put a Christian
construction on what had been a treasured association of his pagan past. Indeed at a later
time we find direct evidence of such a feeling.
Eusebius in his Life of Constantine, written
very shortly after the death of the Emperor in
337, speaks of 'the day of salvation which coincides with that of light and the sun.'[1] A com-
mentary on the Psalms, which appears in
Jerome's works, though it is generally believed
to be spurious, on the verse in the 118th Psalm,
'this is the day which the Lord hath made,' has

[1] *Vita Constantini*, iv, 18, 3.

the following comment: 'The Lord's day, the
day of the Resurrection, the day of Christians,
our day. Why is it called the Lord's day? Because on it he ascended victoriously to his Father.
But if the Gentiles call it the Sun's day, we gladly
admit it. For in this day the light of the world
rose, on this day the sun of righteousness rose.'[1]
In the fifth century Maximus of Turin in a
homily on Pentecost says: 'The Lord's day is
reverenced by us because on it the Saviour of
the world like the rising sun, dispelling the darkness of hell, shone with the light of resurrection,
and therefore is the day called by the men of the
world the Sun's day, because Christ the sun
of righteousness illumines it.'[2] These quotations
belong, as I have said, to a later day. But the fact
on which they are based, the coincidence of the
Christian Lord's day with the pagan Sun's day,
was the same for the men of the first and second
centuries as for those of the fourth and fifth: and
what the Christians of the later epoch wrote may
well have been said and thought by them of the
earlier, even if it was not written; though indeed
it is possible that we have glimpses of the
association in the writings of these earlier times.
I have already noted the thought that may lie behind the words of Ignatius, and it is perhaps
worth noting also that the divine figure which
appears to the seer of the Apocalypse on the

[1] Migne, *Patrologia Latina*, 30, p. 218.
[2] *Ib.* 57, p. 371.

Sun's-day and who holds in his hand the seven
stars has his face 'like the Sun shining in his
strength.' And this brings me to the consideration of two passages in St Paul's letters, the
discussion of which I postponed some pages back.

In Galatians iv, 3, St Paul (referring apparently in the word 'we' to both Jews and
Gentiles) says, 'we, when we were babes, were
enslaved under the *elements of the world*.' A few
verses later he goes on:

> Howbeit at that time, not knowing God, ye were in
> bondage to them which by nature are no gods: but now
> that ye have come to know God, or rather to be known
> of God, how turn ye back again to the weak and beggarly
> *elements*, whereunto ye desire to be in bondage over
> again? Ye observe days and months and seasons and
> years. I am afraid for you, lest by any means I have
> bestowed labour upon you in vain.

Again, in Colossians ii, 8:

> Take heed lest there shall be any one that maketh
> spoil of you through his philosophy and vain deceit, after
> the tradition of men, after the *elements of the world*, and
> not after Christ.... (*v.* 16) Let no man therefore
> judge you in meat, or in drink, or in respect of a feast day
> or a new moon or a sabbath day, which are a shadow of
> the things to come; but the body is Christ's. Let no man
> rob you of your prize by a voluntary humility and wor-
> shipping of the angels.... (*v.* 20) If ye died with Christ
> from the *elements of the world*, why, as though living in
> the world, do ye subject yourselves to ordinances?

The point which concerns us in these passages
is the phrase the 'elements' or the 'elements of

the world.' The word[1] which I have translated
thus is frequently used both for the alphabet (or
rudiments of knowledge) and also in a physical
sense, sometimes for what we call the 'elements,'
but still more for the heavenly bodies, particularly the signs of the Zodiac or the planets.
There has always been much questioning as to
which of these two meanings the word bears in
our passages, but whichever is right must be
right for all four occasions on which it recurs.
Both interpretations can claim high authority
both in ancient and modern times. Our Revised
Version has definitely committed itself to the
first, by translating the word as 'rudiments' in
the body of the text, and relegating the am-
biguous 'elements' of the old Version to the
margin. The main objection to this, to my mind,
is the addition of 'the world' in three out of the
four cases. 'Rudiments of the world' is a strange
expression for an elementary degree of knowledge or enlightenment. But it is perhaps no
stranger than many others in the Pauline epistles,
and I am far from feeling certain that this first
interpretation is wrong. But the second at any
rate deserves careful consideration.

Those who adopt this second explanation
have, I think, generally supposed that Paul
denounces the observation of days, months and
years as bondage to the heavenly bodies, because
we measure time by them. This has always

[1] στοιχεῖα.

seemed to me a very inadequate reason. In this
sense we are all 'in bondage to the elements.'
They bring us winter and summer; they send us
to bed at night and call us up in the morning.
But the interpretation will gain far more force
if we suppose that Paul is thinking mainly of the
planetary week and perhaps also of the other
'chronocratories' by which a planet was lord of
the month or of the year[1]. The devotee of these
planetary chronocratories was really under a
'bondage to the elements' from which those who
held aloof from such observances were free. The
prima facie objection to this hypothesis is that
the errors of the Galatians throughout the epistle
are represented as Judaistic in character. To
justify the suggestion it would be necessary to
suppose that the Galatian Judaism was of a semi-
pagan character and in particular that their Sabbath was partly a Jewish Sabbath and partly a
Saturn's day. But I am not sure that such a
hypothesis is altogether arbitrary. As I have
said above, it is almost a necessity that Jewish
proselytes and indeed Hellenistic Jews should
import into their conceptions of the Sabbath

---

[1] One of the most striking examples quoted by Boll (*v.*
p. 85) from the Apocalypse is ch. ix, 15, 'and the four angels
were loosed, which had been prepared for the hour and day
and month and year, that they should kill the third part of men.'
Those who are convinced otherwise that the book is permeated
by astrology, will naturally find Valens' four chronocratories
here.

some planetary ideas. Indeed, whatever view we take of the doubtful phrase, it is clear that St Paul does regard the Judaism of the Galatians as being to a great extent a return to paganism.

An important link between these two may perhaps be found in the phrase which appears in the parallel passage of the Colossians, where 'worshipping of angels' is one of the errors associated with the bondage to the 'elements of the world.' We not infrequently find hints of the identification of the angels with the stars or planets[1]. In later times we find the seven archangels, whose names were current among the Jews before our era, identified with the seven planets[2]. The analogy indeed is asserted as early as Clement of Alexandria when he says[3] that the first-born and mightiest of the angels are seven,

[1] Thus in the 'Preaching of Peter' quoted by Clement of Alexandria, *Stromateis*, VI (Potter, p. 760), the Jews are accused of worshipping 'angels and archangels, the sun and moon.' Philo, *De Opificio Mundi*, 50 (144), seems to say that the stars are bodies of angels. Compare also *Book of Enoch* (ed. Charles), ch. 86.

[2] *V*. Schürer, p. 21. In the '*Slavonic*' *Enoch* or *Book of the Secrets of Enoch* (edited by Charles and assigned by him to the first century A.D.) we find seven heavens, each with their planet in the normal order just as in Cicero and Dante, and in each of these heavens angels are located, though they are not identified with the planets. Cf. also a curious document in *Cat. Cod. Astr. Graec.* VII, p. 179, where the angels for each day of the week are named.

[3] *Stromateis*, VI (Potter, p. 813)

and seven also the astrologers say are the planets by sympathy with which all mortal things are brought about. And when in the Apocalypse we find in almost the same context seven stars who are angels of the Churches, seven spirits who may or may not be, but were at any rate thought by early fathers to be, the seven archangels, seven candlesticks which are the Churches, and in Josephus and Philo[1] assertions that the seven arms of the great candlestick signified or re-presented the seven planets, we are in touch with an association of ideas, which, however vague and undigested, must in minds, where the ferment of Jewish mysticism and that of planetary observance were working side by side, have led inevitably to a confusion or syncretism of the two. Thus, while I feel by no means certain that in either epistle the phrase 'elements of the world' indicates the planets rather than 'rudimentary teaching,' I do think that we may feel fairly confident that Paul found himself in contact with large bodies of converts with whom angelology was coloured by astrological ideas, and in particular the planetary conception of the week was not felt to be incompatible with the Jewish or Christian conception.

So, as I have said, it was inevitable that belief in the Sun's day should contribute to stereotype the sanctity of the Lord's day. And if we look

[1] Josephus, *Antiquities*, III, 6, 7; Philo, *Quis Rer. Div. Her.* 45 (221).

further we shall see that the process of exhaustion would in itself, by a combination of Jewish and planetary prejudices, have almost settled the choice of this day for the Christian Eucharist, even if there were not, as undoubtedly there were, other considerations. Saturday was impossible not only, as suggested above, through the wish of the Jewish Christian to avoid clashing with the Sabbath, but also through the profound prejudices of the planetist. It might be all very well for the Jew to use Saturn's day for a holy-day, which to the Gentile mind was not the 'Princess Sabbath' as Heine painted it, but served mainly to enforce taboos. It would be a very different matter to celebrate the Eucharist of joy and thanksgiving on a day with such sinister associations. Jupiter is a beneficent planet and Thursday, as being according to the narrative in Acts the day of the Ascension and according to western reckoning of the Last Supper, might have appealed to Christians, but Thursday is a Jewish fast-day, as also is Monday. Mars is like Saturn a sinister planet and this would rule out Tuesday. Mercury, whose day for some reason or other became at an early date a Christian fast-day, is a neutral planet. In fact, the only real competitor of Sunday was Friday.

I have often wondered whether the Church had any feeling of the planetary significance of Friday. On the face of it indeed it might seem that the day of Venus could have little but evil

associations for the Christian, and we have seen
that it has been seriously suggested that Justin
purposely avoids using such a name in connexion
with the day of the Crucifixion. But apart from
the fact that Venus is not always the goddess of
impure love or of sexual love in general—many
will remember the glorious hymn with which
Lucretius opens his great poem and in which he
hails her as the all-generating power of nature
and love—Friday is not, properly speaking, the
day of Venus but of the star of Venus—that most
beautiful and in astrological lore most beneficent of the planets, in eastern countries said
to be visible all day, often ranked with sun and
moon as forming the great triad of the heavens,
the star in fact which is both evening and morning star. Though it is probably true that the
attributes of the planets came to be coloured by
the attributes assigned to their patron deities in
other spheres, strict thought and indeed strict
language did not confuse them. Cicero, for
instance, regularly uses 'stella Mercurii,' 'stella
Martis,' not Mercurius or Mars. All five, indeed, had in early Greek usage non-divine
names. Mercury was Stilbon or the 'twinkler,'
Mars Pyroeis or the 'fiery' one, Jupiter Phaethon
or the shining one, Saturn Phaenon meaning
perhaps the revealer, and Venus was, of course,
Phosphorus the light-bringer or Hesperus the
evening star. The first four of these alternative
names though not entirely lost were largely

superseded by the divine names familiar to us, the
creation, no doubt, of international astrology,
which aimed at giving in each nation the nearest
equivalent for the (presumably) Chaldaean origi-
nals. But Hesper-Phosphor was never superseded. Lists of the planets may be found, where,
while the other divine names are given, there is
no Venus, but Hesperus or Phosphorus. Now
it was on the day of the Evening and Morning
Star that Jesus had, as the Church believed, accomplished His redeeming sacrifice, and indeed
according to the form of reckoning which began
the day at sunset, it was on this day also that
He had instituted the rite which Christians met
weekly to celebrate. Was the Christian imagination stirred by this association of their Master
with the day of the Morning and Evening Star,
as it certainly was to some extent by His association with the Sun's day? Not a single line survives, so far as I know, to shew that it was so, and
yet it is difficult to think that its significance was
altogether missed. For we may remember that
while Jesus is never called the Sun in the New
Testament He is called the Morning Star. In
what are almost the closing words of the Revelation comes the announcement 'I am the root
and the offspring of David, the bright, the
Morning Star.' Perhaps, too, we may couple
with this the mysterious phrase in the message
to the Church of Thyatira in the second chapter:
'to him that overcometh and keepeth my words

to the end, I will give him the Morning Star.'[1]
Commentators from early times have often taken
these words to mean 'I will give him myself,'
and though this interpretation seems to me rather
unnatural, it is clear that the 'Morning Star'
here is something very closely connected with
Christ.

The Church might also have put a Christian
interpretation on the double character of the
planet of Friday. Tennyson fell unconsciously
into language curiously suggestive of the Apocalypse when he wrote in *In Memoriam*:

> Sweet Hesper-Phosphor, double name
> For what is one, the first, the last.

And a still more striking association might have
been found. One of the fancies that gathered
round the planet was that as morning star it
shone upon the living, as evening star went
down to shine upon the dead. This thought is
expressed in an epigram attributed to Plato,
best known, perhaps, because Shelley by set-
ting it at the head of his *Adonais* applied it to
Keats:

[1] Bouché-Leclercq, *L'Astrologie Grecque*, p. 607, has an
attractive explanation of these words. The third heaven which
according to the '*Slavonic*' *Enoch* was the place of Paradise
is of course the zone of Venus in the normal astrology and indeed according to 'Enoch' himself. Thus to give the Morning
Star is to give Paradise. He supports this by 2 Cor. xii, 2–4,
where St Paul tells how he was 'caught up as far as the third
heaven and into Paradise.'

Thou wert the morning-star among the living,
    Ere thy fair light had fled.
Now, having died, thou art as Hesperus giving
    New splendour to the dead[1].

The thought might well have been applied to
Good Friday. No idea was dearer to the early
Church than that the Lord passed on the ninth
hour of that day to 'preach to the spirits in
prison' and to 'harrow hell,' an idea which has
left its mark on the Apostles' creed. That Jesus
was in this way evening star to the dead and
morning star to the living when lifted up on the
cross is a conception which might well have
appealed to the convert who came to the Church
fresh from the lore of Hesper-Phosphor.

However, the fact remains that the Church
instinctively chose Sunday and not Friday for
her weekly festival and turned the latter into
a fast-day. This seems to us from long association more than natural. I am not sure that it
really is so. The work of redemption was accomplished and the victory really won on Good
Friday and, apart from the doubtful question
whether the Last Supper and the institution of
the Eucharist was to be held to belong to Thursday or Friday, one line of thought might easily
have looked upon the latter as a day of triumph

---

[1] ἀστὴρ πρὶν μὲν ἔλαμπες ἐνὶ ζώοισιν ἑῷος | νῦν δὲ θανὼν
λάμπεις ἕσπερος ἐν φθιμένοις. (The translation is Shelley's,
though not printed with *Adonais*.)

rather than mourning[1]. In fact the Church has frequently, if not generally, celebrated the festivals of the saints on the days on which they were supposed to have died and entered into Paradise. When she instinctively took a different line in the case of her Master, was she subconsciously influenced by the mystery religions around her, in which the death of the god was treated as an occasion for mourning and his resurrection hailed with joy? Possibly so. But I should rather incline to think that the rival claims of Sunday and Friday were so closely balanced both on planetary and historical grounds, that the question was decided by some early convenience of usage which grew into a permanent institution, because from both points of view it would find adequate, if not overwhelming, grounds to support it.

There is one more consideration which I wish to put before my readers. Not only is it probable that the planetary week contributed to fix the day of the Christian assembly on one particular day of the seven, but we may also fairly ask whether it is not partly responsible for the recurrence of this Lord's day at intervals of seven days, or, in other words, for the fact that we have a week at all. When the Christian Church abrogated the Sabbath, it really

---

[1] Compare the most famous of the passion hymns, the 'Pange Lingua':

> Pange, lingua, gloriosi praelium certaminis,
> et super crucis tropaeum dic triumphum nobilem.

destroyed the *raison d'être* of the week. It is true
that later Sabbatarianism has developed a doctrine, that though the day has been changed, the
obligation to set apart one day in seven for religious observance is of divine institution. Such
a doctrine might perhaps be reconciled with
the vaguer conception of Sabbatical obligation
which we find in Deuteronomy, but hardly with
the law as laid down in Genesis ii and Exodus xx,
at any rate in the eyes of Jews and Christians.
They must have believed that the seventh day's
rest had gone on continuously from the beginning, or, in other words, that the number of
days which had elapsed between the beginning
of the first day of creation and the end of any
particular Sabbath was an exact multiple of
seven. To assemble on the $7x + 1$th day instead
of on the $7x$th is not to keep the Sabbath, and
the choice lay between keeping it on the proper
day or not at all. Now it would have been per-
fectly compatible with the Pauline view of the
law to take the former alternative. Paul might
well have argued, as our Lord argued of the in-
dissolubility of marriage, that the Sabbath was
not of Moses' institution, but was from the
beginning, and the fact that it alone of the cere-
monial ordinances of the law has a place in the
Decalogue, a point which no doubt has had
great weight in modern feeling, would have confirmed this. But as a matter of fact, though Paul
no doubt retained the Sabbath for himself, as

he did the rest of the law, he repudiated it for his Gentile converts with something like horror to the Galatians and with something like contempt, or at any rate indifference, to the Colossians. And there is not, so far as I know, a syllable in the early Fathers which suggests that the Church refused to follow his lead in this matter. But to the Jew a week is only the interval between two Sabbaths and apart from this no sanctity attaches to it. Why then did the Christian Church continue to hold its meetings weekly, instead of accommodating them to other time measurements such as the Roman *nundinatio*[1] or the numerous sporadic holidays? The answer is because it had imbibed the habit of thinking in terms of seven-day cycles. When it was composed mainly of Jews or those who approached it through the medium of Judaism it was natural enough that the Lord's day should recur every seventh day. But when the Gentile became the overwhelming element, one may doubt whether this practice, which could hardly be said to have apostolic authority, would have maintained itself, if the world had known no seven-day cycle apart from Judaism. The fact then is, I believe, that we owe our religious and civil Sunday to the combination of these two factors, the immemorial familiarity of the Jewish Christian with the Sabbatical week and the recent familiarity of the Gentile Christian with the planetary week.

[1] *V.* note on p. 64.

7

THE WEEK IN NORTHERN EUROPE

The question of when, how and under what influence the week diffused itself in Northern Europe is one on which we have little knowledge beyond the precarious inferences which may be drawn from the names. Welsh has a complete set of Roman planetary names. It stands in fact alone in this respect among European languages. Saturday is *Dydd-sadwrn*, Sunday *Dydd-sul*, Monday *Dydd-llun*. There has been no tendency to supplant the first two of these, as in Latin Europe by *Dominica* and *Sabbatum*, nor again have *Sol* and *Luna* been replaced by the Celtic equivalents for Sun and Moon. The natural inference is that the week spread through the Romanized element in Britain, as it did through the rest of the Empire, under planetary rather than Christian influence, and that the names, now become mere names, then found their way into the vernacular. The later isolation of Britain from the sphere of Roman Christianity will, I imagine, give a quite satisfactory explanation why the Church influence which established the 'Lord's day' so firmly in the south was not so effective in this country.

In the other two great branches of Celtic speech, the Gaelic and the Irish, things took a different course. Monday, Tuesday and Saturday are the days of Luna, Mars and Saturn, but Sunday is Di-domhnaich, and the three other names are formed on quite another principle. The name for Wednesday means 'the first fast,' Friday is 'the fast' or 'the great fast,' while Thursday is something which is variously interpreted as 'the eve of the fast,' 'the second fast,' or 'the day between the fasts,' but at any rate has some such connexion. Here again it is a natural conjecture that the week reached these tribes which lay outside Roman civilization at a later period and in the wake of Christianity. The names for Wednesday, Thursday and Friday distinctly suggest this, that for Sunday is obviously compatible with it, and those for Monday and Tuesday do not suggest the contrary. For as we have seen, the ordinary Christian of the south, if not the strict churchman, continued to use the planetary names for these two. Saturday is indeed a difficulty on this hypothesis. Perhaps we may account for it partly by the influence of their Welsh kinsmen, partly on the supposition that *sabbatum*, though the accepted ecclesiastical name, had not the sanctity of *dominica* and was less likely to be pressed by the Church on the converted or semi-converted population. But all these inferences from names are, as I have said, precarious, and I put them forward rather as theses for consideration than as settled conclusions.

The history of the week-names among the Teutonic nations presents a more important and perplexing problem. We see that the first day is named as in the planetary week from the Sun. The Teuton like the Briton does not accept the Christian alternative of the Lord's day, but unlike the Briton he translates the word *sol* into its Teutonic equivalent. The second day is as elsewhere called after the Moon, and here too the word 'luna' has been translated, not taken over, as it stands, as in Welsh. The third in its various forms can be traced back to a Teutonic deity, whom we may presume and indeed know to have been held as an equivalent of Mars. The fourth in German is merely 'mid-week,' but in English, Dutch and the Scandinavian languages evidently retains the name of Woden or Odin, whom we have reason to think the Romans who were interested in Teutonic mythology identified with their own Mercury. The fifth bears the names of Thunor or Thor, a reasonable equivalent for Jupiter, and the goddess Frigg, who everywhere gives her name to the sixth, is an equally natural representation of Venus. The seventh has become in German Samstag, presumably a corruption of Sabbatum, but in English and Dutch it presents unmistakably Saturn's day, and in this case alone is the name

taken over untranslated[1]; while among the Scan-
dinavians both the pagan and Christian names
are absent, and we have nothing but a word,
which in its various forms means 'washing-
day,' or, as a middle-class Englishman of the
last generation might have said, 'Tub-night.'[2]
Now it is true that we first find these names in
later Christian writers speaking of the heathen
whom they had converted or with whom they
came in contact, but it is obvious that they
represent or are the equivalents of the Roman
planetary week-names and almost equally

[1] Earlier authorities (e.g. the art. on 'Calendar' in the
Enc. Brit.) postulated a Teutonic deity Seterne, but this seems
to be pure invention.

[2] Danish *Loverdag*; *v.* Appendix, p. 117. Professor Chadwick has pointed out to me an interesting illustration of this.
The chronicler John of Wallingford (died 1214), in
describing the massacre of the Danes by Ethelred, says that 'the
Danes had occupied the best parts of East Anglia and that it
was their custom to comb their hair every day, to change their
clothes frequently and *bathe on Saturdays* (*sabbatis balneare*)
and improve their outward appearance by many such frivoli-
ties. Hence they were a snare to the chastity of the English
matrons and had many daughters of nobles for their concu-
bines.' Ethelred was thus induced to consent to the fatal massacre of St Brice's day, Nov. 13th, 1002, and for this, according
to John, Saturday, as their bathing day, was chosen.
Freeman, *Norman Conquest*, I, p. 65, commenting on this
story, says that though John does not mention St Brice's day, that
day did fall on Saturday in 1002. But he is mistaken in this:
it was actually Friday, and as there appears to be no question
as to the accuracy of the date, this part of John's story must be
untrue. I leave to experts to consider how far this invalidates
the earlier part.

obvious that they must have been introduced while
the Teutonic world was still pagan, and through
pagan not Christian influence. If Augustine's
English converts had only known the week, as
presented to them in a Christian form, it is quite
conceivable that they should pick up these pagan
names for five days of the week, which, as the
present week-day names in the Latin countries
shew, remained in general currency, but in this
case we should expect that they would have been
taken over as they stood, with merely linguistic
variations. But it is hardly conceivable that these
converts should have proceeded to turn these
mere survivals of a pagan terminology into the
names of the deities whom they were in the act
of discarding. It is hardly less unintelligible
that they should go one better than their con-
verters and turn the Lord's day back into the
Sun's day and in some countries at any rate
Sabbath into Saturn's day. The conclusion[1]
seems inevitable that the week was carried into
the lands beyond the Rhine and Danube from
the still unchristianized Empire, that is to say,
not much later and probably earlier than the
fourth century. It is quite possible that the
remarkably strong Mithraistic zeal which, as inscriptions shew, prevailed in the Roman army
may have had something to do with this. At any
rate it seems clear to me, that when the week
originally obtained a footing outside the borders

[1] This was also Grimm's opinion.

of the Empire it must have been as a religious institution of some kind. For the argument used above about the changes of the names applies here also. If the week had been accepted as a form of time-measurement current among their more civilized neighbours and therefore worthy of imitation, or for commercial purposes, the names would have been taken over as they stood and not converted into those of Teutonic deities. At the same time it is difficult to suppose that this religious motive had the astrological character which belonged to week-observance when it first spread within the Empire. There does not seem to be the slightest trace of these astrological ideas in what we know of Teutonic mythology, or any hint that the deities had any connexion with the planets. Furthermore, we have to account for the fact that the system with its non-Latin names was not only introduced but preserved during the considerable and obscure gap between the latest time at which it can have been introduced and the date at which it re-appears, when it comes into contact with Christianity. For that it was so preserved is clear. Augustine's Kentish converts when they were bidden to hear Mass on the Lord's day already knew it as the Sun's day. What were the ideas that preserved it? To those who think that a seven-day continuous cycle is so natural and valuable a way of time-measurement that it will preserve itself automatically the question will seem superfluous.

I have already given my reasons for thinking the contrary. I can only suppose that one or more of the days preserved some civil or religious significance during this interval. But what this was we can only guess. One hint only I have found. Grimm notes that some special observance continued to be paid for centuries in Central Europe to Thursday[1]. This can hardly be a Christian growth, as we might have thought in the case of Sunday or Friday, and it looks like an indication that the Teutonic world, having taken the week-day names from their neighbours and having identified first the planet of Jupiter with the god Jupiter and then the latter with their own thunder-god, came to believe that he needed propitiation once in seven days. This in itself was bound to preserve the week-cycle, even if no other observance attached itself to the other six. But in all this section it must be remembered that I am speaking without the special knowledge that can lend authority to conjecture[2]. It would obviously be impossible to conclude my investigation of the planetary week without some mention of at any rate the Teutonic adoption of it. But I can do little more than state a case in

[1] *Teutonic Mythology* (Eng. trans.), I, p. 191. The evidence after the eighth century or so does not seem very strong, and I should add that Professor Chadwick considers the suggestion somewhat fanciful.

[2] Though I am glad to say that so high an authority as Professor Chadwick has read the pages on the Teutonic week and does not raise any objection, except that just mentioned.

the hope that those who are specialists in Celtic or Teutonic mythology and antiquities may give it a consideration which I do not think it has yet received.

I have been obliged to end, as I began, on a note of uncertainty, and it may also be said that much of the intermediate part, particularly as to the relation between the Christian Church and the planetary week, is somewhat conjectural. But there is a great difference between the two forms of uncertainty. In the one—that which besets the question of the existence of the prehistoric week and the meaning of the Teutonic week—we suffer from a paucity of facts. In the case of the other we have abundance of facts, though the inferences to be drawn from them may be doubtful. But, apart from these two conjectural elements, there is much which is certainly historical. That our week rests upon a combination of the Jewish and the planetary week, that the latter obtained a remarkable currency during the first two centuries A.D., and that it is in origin an hour rather than a day system, are truths to my mind established beyond question. If this little treatise falls into the hands of what are called 'general readers,' experience tells me that to the great majority the matter will be new, and if they fail to find it interesting, I shall conclude that it is my method of presenting the subject, rather than the subject itself, which is at fault.

APPENDIX

A

Week-day names in various European languages

1) French	Italian	Spanish	Portuguese
Dimanche	Domenica	Domingo	Domingo
Lundi	Lunedi	Lunes	Segunda Feira
Mardi	Martedi	Martes	Terça "
Mercredi	Mercoledi	Miercoles	Quarta "
Jeudi	Giovedi	Jueves	Quinta "
Vendredi	Venerdi	Viernes	Sexta "
Samedi	Sabato	Sabado	Sabado

(2) Dutch	German	Danish	Norwegian and
Zondag	Sonntag	Sondag	Swedish much
Maandag	Montag	Mandag	the same
Dinsdag	Dienstag	Tirsdag	
Woensdag	Mittwoch	Onsdag	
Dondersdag	Donnerstag	Torsdag	
Vrijdag	Freitag	Fredag	
Zaterdag	Samstag	Loverdag	

(3) Welsh	Gaelic	Irish
Dydd-sul	Di-domhnaich	Much the same
Dydd-llun	Di-luain	
Dydd-mawrth	Di-mairt	
Dydd-mercher	Di-ciadain	
Dydd-iou	Diar-daoin	
Dydd-gwener	Di-h-aoine	
Dydd-sadwrn	Di-sathirne	

(4) Russian	Polish	Czech	Hungarian
Voskresénie (also Nedélya)	Niedziela	Nedele	Vasarnap
Ponedelnik	Poniedzialek	Pondeli	Hetfo
Vtornik	Wtorek	Uterek(j)	Kedd
Sredá	Środa	Strèda	Szerda
Chetvérg	Czwartek	Čtvrtek	Csötörtök
Pyátnitsa	Piatek	Pátek	Pentek
Subbota	Sobota	Sobota	Szombat

(5) *Modern Greek*	(6) *Albanian*
κυριακή	Dielli
δευτέρα	Hanε
τρίτη	Martε
τετάρτη	Merkurrε
πέμπτη	Enjετε
παρασκευή	Premtε
σάββατον	Shtunε

Most of the remarks that need to be made on the first three groups will be found in the preceding pages. In the first or Latin group, the most noticeable point is the dropping of the five planetary names in Portugal and their replacement by numerical terms, or in other words the complete adoption of the regular ecclesiastical nomenclature. In the second or Teutonic group the chief variations are those concerned with the seventh day (*v.* pp. 110, 111). Kinship of tongue and obvious identity of origin in some of the names makes it natural to class the three Celtic languages of Group 3 together, but I have already pointed out on p. 109 the vital differences between the Welsh and the other two.

The fourth or Slavonic group has not hitherto been dealt with. The ordinary Russian name for Sunday means 're-surrection.' Those for Tuesday, Thursday and Friday in all three languages mean respectively 'second,' 'fourth' and 'fifth,' that for Wednesday means 'middle,' like the German 'Mittwoch.' 'Subbota' or 'Sobota' is obviously 'Sabbath,' as in most European languages. The variant in Russia for Sunday, 'Nedélya,' which is said to be used in South Russian dialects, is, it will be seen, the regular name in Polish and Czech, and its original meaning is 'not working.' In all three languages it is also the ordinary term for the week in general—clearly a secondary use exactly analogous to the New Testament use of 'Sabbata' for week as well as Sabbath. Since 'po' means 'after' we see that 'Monday' is expressed as the 'day after the non-working day.' This helps to explain a curious feature in the Slavonic terminology. The fact that Tuesday, Thursday and Friday are spoken of as the second, fourth and fifth days instead of third, fifth and sixth, shews that the week is thought of as beginning on Monday.

This is a natural idea from the point of view of the worker, who conceives of the rest-day as following his working-days. But it is entirely opposed to ecclesiastical and biblical usage. It is thus in marked contrast with the strong religious feeling expressed in the ordinary Russian name of 'Resurrection-day' for Sunday.

Hungarian or Magyar is not a Slavonic nor indeed an Indo-European language; but the names of the last four days have every appearance of an identical origin with those of their Slavonic neighbours. The name for Monday may perhaps mean 'beginning of the week.' But I have not met with any expert in the language who could assure me of this or interpret the other two names.

In Group 5 the meaning of the names is obvious to any one who has the slightest knowledge of Greek. But for the benefit of those who have not, I may add that they are Lord's-day, second, third, fourth, fifth, Preparation and Sabbath. The name for Friday is of course the biblical name, which is regularly used by the Greek Fathers. The reader will note the point already mentioned on p. 26 that the Eastern Church succeeded generally if not entirely in suppressing the planetary names.

Albanian (Group 6) is an Indo-European language, but of a family distinct from either Italian or Greek. Here I have had the advantage of consulting one who has made a considerable study of the language, Dr B. Atkinson, as well as of a discussion by Dr A. Thumb in the article mentioned on p. 45. The names so far as we can interpret them are purely planetary. Those for Sunday and Monday are the *vernacular* words for 'sun' and 'moon,' which shews that the names were not mere borrowings, but had a meaning for the Albanians. Tuesday and Wednesday speak for themselves, and the equivalence of 'Shtunɛ' and 'Saturn' though not free from philological difficulty seems probable. The other two are mysterious. 'Enjɛtɛ,' it has been suggested, may come from the name of a local deity sometimes identified with Zeus. 'Prɛmtɛ' is supposed by some scholars to be akin to the Albanian word for 'evening.' If this is accepted, two explanations would be possible: (1) that it means 'eve' or 'vigil' and is the equivalent of the Church term 'preparation'; (2) that we have here the other name for Venus, 'Hesperus' or 'evening-star,' *v.* p. 102. The freedom from Church influence shewn in the other names tends to support the latter.

B

The Week and the Four Phases of the Moon (*v.* pp. 2, 3)

The question whether these were originally connected is discussed by Boll (article on 'Hebdomad' in Pauly-Wissowa, *Real-cycl.* VII, 2551), and Nilsson (*v.* Note C, p. 330). Boll adduces several passages from Varro, Philo, Clement and others where it is assumed that the moon completes its circuit in four periods of seven days each. The earliest and therefore the most important of these is a Babylonian 'Creation Epic,' in which the Creator addresses the moon as follows: 'At the beginning of the month shine in the land. Beam with thy horns, to make known six days. On the seventh day halve thy disc. On the fourteenth thou shalt reach the half of the monthly growth.' (The rest is lost or at least does not indicate the days.) The question however is whether this loose idea of the moon's movements has produced the septenary arrangement, or (as Nilsson argues) been produced by it. In Babylonia, as has been stated, the seventh, fourteenth, twenty-first and twenty-eighth were marked days, that is to say the months had been subdivided into periods in which seven predominated, or in other words they had what I have called lunar weeks, though not that very different thing, the continuous week. When this has once been done, the septenary periods are for practical purposes so near to the lunar phases, that the latter are in popular language expressed in terms of the former. I think we should all to-day follow this practice and speak of the full-moon as coming a 'fortnight' after the new moon.

C

The Jewish Week and Sabbath

Since the main body of this book was in type, I have come across some discussion of the above subject in a work on *Primitive Time-Reckoning* by the Swedish professor Martin P. Nilsson (English translation, Oxford University Press). He mentions but does not accept a theory which has received some favourable consideration in Germany that the Sabbath was originally and up to the time of the Exile a Full-moon festival. While he writes very cautiously he inclines to the view that it was originally a market-day. Primitive time-reckoning shews many such market-weeks (pp. 333 ff. and for examples the previous pages). They are of three, four, five, six, eight and ten days. 'The market-day is a rest-day, since the people go to market; since they rest and gather together it is therefore a festival….The development of market and rest-day into a day of taboo is everywhere natural and is attested in the above examples from Africa.' He adds that it is an accident that we do not find any other example of a seven-day week of this kind.

The word 'accident' prompts me to take the opportunity of making one point clear. Throughout I have taken the view that the Jewish Week and the Planetary Week, though they met and became intertwined round about the time of our era, are distinct in origin. I may seem thus to have treated the fact that they both consisted of *seven* days as an accident or coincidence. But coincidences are open to suspicion. And those who still conceive of the week as an immemorial institution taking different associations and forms of nomenclature at different times, may feel that this 'coincidence' is for them and against me. Therefore let me add that I would so far modify the word as to admit that in both cases the number may be due to the number of the planets. The Planetary Week is obviously based *directly* on it. The Jewish Week may be *indirectly* based on it; that is to say the number of the planets may well have contributed to consecrate the number seven, and this sense of consecration may have led the Israelitish mind to make each rest-day or market-day the seventh from the preceding one. I have implied this already on pp. 4 and 56, but feel that a definite statement of it here may disarm some criticism.

D

Additional Note to p. 19

It is worth noting that not only does Cicero so far vacillate about the order of the planets, that in one place he puts Venus below Mercury, but this order is also given by Philo (*Quis Rer. Div. Her.* 45 (224)) who declares his preference for it, though he states that others have been suggested. As Philo lived some 80 years after Cicero, the statement on p. 19 that the order on which the week hour-system was based, which I have called the normal order, was the *accepted* order from the second century B.C. requires perhaps some modification. And this also has some bearing on the value of Dion's statement that the planetary week emanated from Egypt. For Dion also calls the 'normal order' the 'order accepted by the Egyptians' (*v.* p. 44). If the belief in this order was especially characteristic of Egypt, it is strange that the Alexandrian scholar should give a different one.

It will be seen that an hour-cycle with Mercury in the fifth place and Venus in the sixth, would produce a day-cycle with Mercury in the sixth and Venus in the fourth place, or in other words Wednesday and Friday would change places. It is perhaps possible that this form of the Planetary Week may have been current for some time side by side with the form that has survived. There is nothing in any evidence existing for the Planetary Week (*v.* pp. 32–35), till we come to the discoveries at Pompeii, which would forbid this.

E

Text of the passage in Dion Cassius XXXVII, 18
translated on pp. 21–22 and 43–44

καὶ τὰ μὲν κατ' ἐκεῖνον, τίς τε ἔστι καὶ ὅθεν οὕτως
ἐτιμήθη, ὅπως τε περὶ αὐτὸν ἐπτόηνται, πολλοῖς τε εἴρηται
καὶ οὐδὲν τῇδε τῇ ἱστορίᾳ προσήκει· τὸ δὲ δὴ ἐς τοὺς ἀστέρας
τοὺς ἑπτὰ τοὺς πλανήτας ὠνομασμένους τὰς ἡμέρας ἀνακεῖσθαι
κατέστη μὲν ὑπ' Αἰγυπτίων, πάρεστι δὲ καὶ ἐπὶ πάντας ἀνθρώ-
πους οὐ πάλαι ποτὲ ὡς λόγῳ εἰπεῖν ἀρξάμενον· οἱ γοῦν ἀρχαῖοι
Ἕλληνες οὐδαμῇ αὐτό, ὅσα γε ἐμὲ εἰδέναι, ἠπίσταντο. ἀλλ'
ἐπειδὴ καὶ πάνυ νῦν τοῖς τε ἄλλοις ἅπασι καὶ αὐτοῖς τοῖς
Ῥωμαίοις ἐπιχωριάζει, καὶ ἤδη καὶ τοῦτό σφισι πάτριον τρόπον
τινά ἐστι, βραχύ τι περὶ αὐτοῦ διαλεχθῆναι βούλομαι, πῶς τε
καὶ τίνα τρόπον οὕτω τέτακται. ἤκουσα δὲ δύο λόγους ἄλλως
μὲν οὐ χαλεποὺς γνωσθῆναι, θεωρίας δέ τινος ἐχομένους. εἰ γάρ
τις τὴν ἁρμονίαν τὴν διὰ τεσσάρων καλουμένην, ἥπερ που καὶ
τὸ κῦρος τῆς μουσικῆς συνέχειν πεπίστευται, καὶ ἐπὶ τοὺς
ἀστέρας τούτους, ὑφ' ὧν ὁ πᾶς τοῦ οὐρανοῦ κόσμος διείληπται,
κατὰ τὴν τάξιν, καθ' ἣν ἕκαστος αὐτῶν περιπορεύεται, ἐπαγάγοι
καὶ ἀρξάμενος ἀπὸ τῆς ἔξω περιφορᾶς τῆς τῷ Κρόνῳ δεδομένης,
ἔπειτα διαλιπὼν δύο τὰς ἐχομένας τὸν τῆς τετάρτης δεσπότην
ὀνομάσειε καὶ μετ' αὐτὸν δύο αὖ ἑτέρας ὑπερβὰς ἐπὶ τὴν
ἑβδόμην ἀφίκοιτο, καὶ τῷ αὐτῷ τούτῳ τρόπῳ αὐτάς τε ἐπιὼν
καὶ τοὺς ἐφόρους σφῶν θεοὺς ἀνακυκλῶν ἐπιλέγοι ταῖς ἡμέραις,
εὑρήσει πάσας αὐτὰς μουσικῶς πως τῇ τοῦ οὐρανοῦ διακοσμήσει
προσηκούσας. εἰς μὲν δὴ οὗτος λέγεται λόγος, ἕτερος δὲ ὅδε.
τὰς ὥρας τῆς ἡμέρας καὶ τῆς νυκτὸς ἀπὸ τῆς πρώτης ἀρξάμενος
ἀριθμεῖν καὶ ἐκείνην μὲν τῷ Κρόνῳ διδούς, τὴν δὲ ἔπειτα τῷ
Διὶ καὶ τρίτην Ἄρει, τετάρτην ἡλίῳ, πέμπτην Ἀφροδίτῃ,
ἕκτην Ἑρμῇ καὶ ἑβδόμην σελήνῃ κατὰ τὴν τάξιν τῶν κύκλων,
καθ' ἣν οἱ Αἰγύπτιοι αὐτὴν νομίζουσι, καὶ τοῦτο καὶ αὖθις
ποιήσας, πάσας γὰρ οὕτω τὰς τέσσαρας καὶ εἴκοσιν ὥρας
περιελθὼν εὑρήσεις τὴν πρώτην τῆς ἐπιούσης ἡμέρας ὥραν
ἐς τὸν ἥλιον ἀφικνουμένην. καὶ τοῦτο καὶ ἐπ' ἐκείνων τῶν
τεσσάρων καὶ εἴκοσιν ὡρῶν κατὰ τὸν αὐτὸν τοῖς πρόσθεν λόγον

πράξας τῇ σελήνῃ τὴν πρώτην τῆς τρίτης ἡμέρας ὥραν ἀνα-
θήσεις, κἂν οὕτω καὶ διὰ τῶν λοιπῶν πορεύῃ, τὸν προσήκοντα
ἑαυτῇ θεὸν ἑκάστη ἡμέρα λήψεται.

F

(v. p. 35 note)

Horace, *Sat.* II, 3, 288–292 has the following:

> 'Iuppiter, ingentes qui das adimisque labores'
> mater ait pueri menses iam quinque cubantis
> 'frigida si puerum quartana reliquerit, illo
> mane die, quo tu indicis ieiunia, nudus
> in Tiberi stabit.'

('Jupiter, who givest and removest heavy trouble,' says
the mother of the child who has lain on a sick bed for five
months, 'if the chill quartan ague leave my child, on that
morning on which thou enjoinest a fast, he shall stand naked
in the Tiber.')

This passage in which Horace is satirising superstition
as a form of madness is sometimes supposed to shew week
usage, on the authority of the commentator Porphyrio, who
gives as an explanation of 'illo die' 'dies Iovis,' meaning
no doubt Thursday. The fact that Thursday was a Jewish
fast-day might be adduced as an additional argument; and
it seems to be true that we know of no regular 'ieiunia Iovis'
in these times, as there were 'ieiunia Cereris.'

Nevertheless the idea does not seem to me to have any
real foundation, for: (1) Though Porphyrio's date is vague,
he certainly lived at a time when the name of 'Jupiter's day'
had come into general use and it was not unnatural that
he should interpret the phrase in this way. If we knew that
he got the interpretation from any of the earliest commentators, the case would of course be different. (2) Horace is
clearly not thinking of Jewish superstitions such as he satirises
elsewhere. This is shewn by the address to Jupiter in line 288,
and a few lines further down he speaks of the mother as
actuated by 'fear of the Gods.' (3) On the other hand

supposing he knew the planetary week, it is not likely that he would have any reason for supposing that those who observed it would regard 'Jupiter's day' as a fast-day. Jupiter as I have often said is a beneficent planet.

Anyhow, even if the allusion to Thursday is accepted, it will not bring us to a substantially, if at all, earlier date than the Tibullus passage (*v*. p. 35). The second book of the *Satires* was written in or about the year 30 B.C.

G

The name 'Lord's-day' (κυριακή)

A good deal has been written about the origin of this name, and it has sometimes been suggested that it was formed on the analogy of the name σεβαστή, i.e. Augustan, given as we learn from inscriptions and papyri to different days in Egypt and elsewhere, presumably in honour of the emperor. Mention of these 'Augustan days' is very common in the first century. The idea that the name suggested to the Christians a title for their own meeting-day, was, I think, originally a consequence of another conjecture, viz. that the σεβασταί were the first days of each month. Further discoveries however shew that they were quite sporadic, and I believe that no one has yet found any principle which governs their distribution.

I see no reason to go outside Christian thought to account for the name Lord's-day. As we find the Eucharist called by St Paul the Lord's Supper (κυριακὸν δεῖπνον), and as one of the chief purposes, indeed *the* chief purpose of the Christian meeting was to celebrate this, nothing seems to me more natural than that the day should also be called κυριακή.

One point in connexion with the σεβασταί may be mentioned here. A theory has been put forward by Deissmann and others that they were some particular day of the week. (Deissmann for some reason unknown to me selected Thursday.) Those who suggested this might have reflected that

---

the hypothesis is easily tested. The name σεβαστή is often appended in the Papyri to particular days in which both the month and year are given. As we have exact knowledge of the Egyptian reformed calendar (*v.* p. 52), we can in these cases easily ascertain the week-day. I may take two or three examples from Grenfell and Hunt's *Oxyrynchus Papyri*, vol. ii (*v.* Index iii). Thus we find the following days described as σεβασταί:

A.D. 41 Neos Sebastos 20 = Nov. 16th (Thursday)
A.D. 56 Payni 20 = June 14th (Monday)
A.D. 57 Germanicus 18 = May 13th (Friday)

H

Early Christian view of the Sabbath
(*v.* p. 107)

For what seems to me a clear as well as learned discussion of the subject, I refer my readers to Hussey's Bampton Lectures (1860) on 'Sunday.'

For EU product safety concerns, contact us at Calle de José Abascal, 56–1°,
28003 Madrid, Spain or eugpsr@cambridge.org.

www.ingramcontent.com/pod-product-compliance
Ingram Content Group UK Ltd.
Pitfield, Milton Keynes, MK11 3LW, UK
UKHW020313140625
459647UK00018B/1858